Parent Programs in Reading: Guidelines for Success

by
Anthony D. Fredericks
Catasauqua, Pennsylvania, Area School District
and
David Taylor
Moravian College

Published by the
INTERNATIONAL READING ASSOCIATION
800 Barksdale Road   Box 8139   Newark, Delaware 19714

INTERNATIONAL READING ASSOCIATION

Copyright 1985 by the
International Reading Association, Inc.

Library of Congress Cataloging in Publication Data

Fredericks, Anthony D.
    Parent programs in reading.

    Bibliography: p.
    1. Domestic education. 2. Reading. 3. Home and
school. I. Taylor, David, 1950- . II. Title.
LC37.F74 1985   649'.58   85-851
ISBN 0-87207-965-1

Contents

iii

ACKNOWLEDGEMENTS

A book of this scope would not have been possible without the support and contributions of a number of people. The authors are deeply indebted to these individuals for their insight and input to this work. To Elaine Gardner and Cathy Snyder for "energizing" many of the initial ideas; to Carol Turozci, Barb Dreas, and Gretchen Krasley for sharing their thoughts and suggestions; Chris Fredericks, Peggy Barnes, and Lee Foster who added a depth and focus to these ideas during the Preconvention Institute in Anaheim; to Joan Elliott of Indiana University of Pennsylvania and John Wood of Kutztown University who unselfishly provided necessary materials; Phyllis Disher Fredericks for her illustrations; Diane Taylor for her assistance; and the word processing staff at Moravian College—Jean Hunter, Jean Siska, Micki Ortiz, and Catherine Cruciani—who were invaluable in the preparation of this manuscript.

iv

Foreword

Effective use of a child's first teacher is essential if classroom teachers are to provide necessary reading experiences. This publication, *Parent Programs in Reading: Guidelines for Success*, presents a step-by-step procedure for teachers, supervisors, and administrators to use as they initiate or refine a parental involvement program.

This practical guide offers suggestions for determining the need for involving parents in your school. Based on this individual school profile, ideas for implementation are provided. Excellent possibilities for publicity of parent programs are included along with examples of successful parent programs. The appendix of materials and activities should be most helpful as such programs are developed.

Parent Programs in Reading: Guidelines for Success is a practical resource book which represents a significant addition to the libraries of those interested in using parents to enrich their reading program.

Martha D. Collins
Louisiana State University

Preface

Involving parents in the reading curriculum has been one way for teachers, reading specialists, and administrators to foster a unity between home and school. Their efforts are based in part on a growing body of research that documents the significant effect parents can have on their child's reading achievement in school (Burgess, 1982; Henderson, 1981; Hickey et al., 1979; Siders and Sledjeski, 1978; Vukelich, 1978; Vukelich & Naeny, 1980). Yet, despite the vital interest in making parents members of the reading team, there remains a lack of reliable information about beginning and carrying out parent programs. Educators need the "how to's" of successful guidelines, techniques, and strategies for bringing parents into the process of their child's growth in reading. The purpose of this book is to meet the need for realistic, step-by-step plans that are based on a workable model of a parent program.

Readers are first presented with the Preprogram Survey, an informal assessment of attitudes and skills that are important in parent programs. A book such as this one can provide educators with suggested activities and procedures. But those suggestions are useless until matched with an individual's initiative, interest, and skills—all of which are necessary for a program to thrive.

Chapter 1 contains the Parent Reading Engagement Profile (PREP), a four stage paradigm which provides a way to coordinate the elements of an effective program. The profile offers guidelines and examples for needs assessment, program planning, program implementation, and evaluation—the basic construction of most parent projects.

Publicity and promotion are the topics of Chapter 2. Since effective programs engage all parts of the school community, educators need ways to inform people about a program and to encourage parents to participate.

Chapter 3 presents a brief overview of a variety of parent programs and projects that have been successfully implemented in different educational settings. These sample programs include those based in the home and in the school, as well as projects that combine elements of both. We hope that a presentation of them will encourage readers to adapt programs for their own use.

Following the discussion of model programs is an appendix of materials and activities that have been used in some of these programs. As before, the hope is that readers can make good use of them to design and carry out their program that taps the considerable educational potential of parents working with teachers in a reading curriculum.

The approach to parent programs in this work is shaped by several basic assumptions:

First, the most successful parent programs in reading are built upon an understanding of the importance of parenting in the lives of children. Parents are viewed as loving, caring individuals capable of providing the best possible social and educational environment for their offspring. Whether children live in a nuclear family, single parent home, or other familial construct, parents or guardians can be a child's first and often most important teacher (Home and School Institute, 1979).

Second, programs that address the needs of parents rather than those of educators have the best chance of success. Parents must believe that a program in reading has at its heart their desires and goals for their children. They must also believe that their participation in the program will directly benefit the scholastic achievement of their children.

Third, effective parent programs are an integrated component of the reading curriculum, not an adjunct service of the school. Parents are not included solely to satisfy the whims of a few or to respond to outside pressures. Rather, parents are seen as important to the individual reading success of each pupil as well as to the program as a whole.

Fourth, to have the greatest effect, parent participation should extend to all levels of the school, including parents of students from kindergarten through twelfth grade (Rich, 1979). In addition, all categories of parents need to be addressed: single parents; working parents; new parents; parents from different ethnic groups; parents of gifted, average, or remedial students; and parents new to the community (Ervin, 1982).

Fifth, all segments of the school community need to be involved in the planning, design, and support of any effective program (Della-Dora, 1979). School board members, administrative staff, professional personnel, as well as parents can all give a sense of vitality and importance to a parent project in reading. Programs that exist in isolation from one or more of these groups limit their scope of involvement and their impact as well.

Sixth, programs should offer, whenever possible, a variety of activities so that all parents have a chance to participate in one or more portions of the program. Narrowly defined programs which address narrowly defined populations are limited in their effectiveness. The modern family is involved in numerous activities, often with both parents working. The crowded schedules of most families demand that effective parent programs today be flexible and varied.

In summary, most successful parent programs reinforce the natural partnership between home and school, one that too often goes unrecognized and unused. But it is this very partnership that can bring a unity to our efforts in helping a child to read successfully and to read for life.

Preprogram Survey

Parental involvement in the reading curriculum can add an exciting dimension to the overall scholastic program. It underscores and reinforces the partnership between home and school that is necessary for academic achievement. But to be both successful and long lasting, it also requires commitment on the part of school personnel.

The following questionnaire provides educators an opportunity to assess their commitment to the philosophy and goals of a parent program in reading. The items suggest most of the attitudes and administrative skills that teachers, reading specialists, administrators, and parents feel are typical of participants in successful parent programs (Ault et al., 1976; Ervin, 1982; Rich et al., 1979; Texas Education Agency, 1979). Taken together, the questions provide a way to determine whether one should undertake this kind of project.

The questionnaire can be completed by placing either *yes* or *no* in front of those statements with which the reader agrees or disagrees. *N* should be put before any statement about which the reader is unsure or neutral. Since this scale is for self-evaluation only, there is no numerical scoring for the responses. However, an answer of yes to a majority of the statements can indicate that the commitment, background, and circumstances required for a successful parent program are present.

This questionnaire can be appropriate for inservice meetings, too. When duplicated and given to colleagues for self-administration, it can identify those most committed to parental involvement – an important step in insuring that the desire and motivation necessary for a successful program are present.

Preprogram Survey

_____   1. I have a sufficient background in reading through graduate studies, independent reading, or attendance at conferences.

_____   2. I am enthusiastic about parent involvement in reading.

_____ 3. I am confident that I can successfully initiate and carry out a program involving parents.

_____ 4. I am willing to accept small beginnings in developing a program.

_____ 5. I am willing to join with parents in a cooperative venture, not necessarily taking the leadership role.

_____ 6. I can enlist the support of the administration in designing, implementing, and carrying out a new program.

_____ 7. I realize that there may be budgetary restrictions for any new project, but believe that I can find ways to work around them.

_____ 8. I can insure that adequate time will be made available to carry out the provisions of a new program.

_____ 9. I can recruit the help and assistance of other staff members.

_____ 10. I can envision the successful cooperation of parents, teachers, and students in improving pupils' reading ability.

_____ 11. I believe that most, if not all, of the parents I deal with can become active participants in their children's reading development.

_____ 12. I believe that I can enlist student support as a vital component of a parent program in reading.

_____ 13. I am willing to make mistakes, to learn from them, and to forge ahead in new directions, if necessary.

_____ 14. I know that the ultimate goal of any parent project is the increased motivation and achievement of students in reading.

Chapter One

Parent Reading Engagement Profile

Overview

The increased emphasis on parent involvement in reading also brings with it the need for thoughtful, step-by-step procedures that can bring about meaningful and long lasting parent participation. Unfortunately, many parent projects in reading suffer because a systematic design was not followed from the beginning. It is often this simple lack of time and care in planning that weakens programs or is the cause of their failure.

The following planning model is one way to meet the need for a coherent and methodical approach to parent programs in reading. Entitled the Parent Reading Engagement Profile (PREP), it is a four stage model designed to engage parents in any reading program. Its four steps of needs assessment, planning, implementation, and evaluation enable an educator to: 1) target the perceived needs and interests of parents, 2) develop appropriate activities and materials, 3) implement those activities and communicate information about them, and 4) evaluate the effectiveness of the program. The Parent Reading Engagement Profile thus offers a plan of action and a chance to establish an interactive network through which educators and families can encourage and support growth in reading.

The accompanying illustration is of the Profile and its four phases. After the discussion of each phase in the following sections, a completed Profile will be given as an example of its possible use. The particular parent reading project developed in the Profile is entitled "Parents and Reading Partners," a program to encourage children and parents to read together for fifteen minutes each day. The development of this program in one elementary school shows how the separate phases of the PREP can be used together and reinforces the need for a systematic approach to parental involvement. Readers may wish to refer to the completed profile for illustration of specific points in the discussion to follow.

Parent Reading Engagement Profile (PREP)

I. NEEDS ASSESSMENT	II. PROGRAM PLANNING
Type　　　　　*Date*	A.　Goals and Objectives
Needs Statements 1. 2. 3.	B.　Proposed Activities C.　Time Line

III. PROGRAM IMPLEMENTATION	IV. EVALUATION	
Responsibilities	*Formal*	*Informal*

	Awareness	Motivation	Evaluation Statements
			1. 2. 3.
	Involvement	Recognition	4.

Fredericks and Taylor

Phase 1: Needs Assessment

Unfortunately, many well-intentioned parent projects in reading never get off the ground, suffer from small enrollments, or fall victim to steadily declining enrollment (Granowsky et al., 1979). Commonplace are comments from educators such as "I worked for six weeks on this parent workshop and nobody showed up." or "We must have sent home at least three letters about this program and we still have only a couple of parents involved." Such remarks, tinged with a note of futility, suggest that parents and educators may not always be meeting on common ground and that even the best intentioned projects are ineffectual if they do not serve the immediate needs of the clients. Simply put, parents are most likely to participate only in those programs that address their specific desires and concerns.

Parent programs in reading often have been based on *assumed* rather than *assessed* needs (Gardner & O'Loughlin-Snyder, 1981). As a result, parents have not always been involved in determining the scope of such projects, nor in establishing the range of their own involvement. Seemingly, many unsuccessful parent programs do not contain what parents really desire but what educators can easily implement. To the contrary, effective parent projects should be based on a thorough and ongoing assessment of what children need and what parents are interested in doing. This needs assessment should measure the difference between a program's current status and its ideal status; thus this phase is crucial in helping to bridge the gap between what is and what could be (Connecticut State Department of Education, 1976).

Assessment of parent needs can take many forms. In fact, assessment which is broadly based, employing a variety of formal and informal devices, will yield the most useful information (Duncan, 1977). Fortunately, there is available to educators a variety of assessment methods that can be of value when beginning a parent program. The uses of these tools and some examples of them are discussed.

Formal Methods of Needs Assessment

1. *Standardized Achievement Tests*. Because they are designed to measure the cognitive growth of students, standardized tests do not indicate the values or needs of parents. However, they do signal the need for a parent's help when a child is having academic difficulty. In addition, cautious interpretation of school or districtwide test results, when they are discussed with parent groups, can generate awareness of reading needs and open the door to the use of other assessment tools.

2. *Questionnaires*. The most popular devices, questionnaires typically employ a free response or precoded answer format that asks respondents to supply their own answers to a set of questions, or to choose one of several preselected answers

to a question. In either format, well-designed questionnaires can provide highly specific and easy to interpret information that is relevant to a given group.

3. *Attitude Scales.* These measure intensity of feelings throughout a preestablished sequence of statements and have the advantage of providing qualitative analysis of parents' feelings about certain aspects of the reading program or about their own educational perceptions. Examples of attitude instruments include semantic differential scales, paired statements, Likert type scales, and projective or incomplete sentence tests (Heathington, 1975).

4. *Checklists.* This form of assessment combines ease of administration with simplicity of interpretation. Statements on a checklist are usually framed in language that the respondents can easily grasp and understand. Thus relatively little time is needed to complete each checklist, an important bonus when respondents may not want to spend the time to complete additional or more involved types of instruments.

5. *Inventories.* These devices are different in that the respondents are free to check statements in which they have an interest or to leave blank and omit others. While interpretation may be more time consuming, the patterns of response can denote traits or form interest trends in the individual or whole group.

6. *Self-Evaluative Scales.* This type of instrument provides useful personal information and thus is appropriate for small groups or specific individuals. The disadvantage of this method, however, is that responses can be reflection of how a person thinks he or she should respond, rather than always an indication of true feelings (Heathington, 1975). Self-evaluative scales should be followed by other devices to assure their validity.

Informal Methods of Needs Assessment

1. *Individual Conferences.* These provide a personal setting in which parents can talk about, on a one-to-one basis, their opinions and desires concerning the reading program. If educators use listening as a conference tool, parents can share their views in an atmosphere of mutual trust and understanding. A common counseling technique can be of help in listening to parents. Psychologists and other kinds of counselors are trained to listen fully to someone without planning a response. After the person is finished speaking, the counselor pauses a few seconds and often tries to paraphrase briefly, to the other person's satisfaction, what was just said. The paraphrase lets the person know that someone was truly listening and accurately understood the emotions or ideas being expressed.

2. *Small Group Discussions.* Because these sessions allow for interaction among group members, participants may share their viewpoints when they find others with similar concerns. One of the leader's tasks is to provide direction for the

group in expressing needs for individual children or for the entire reading program.

3. *Telephone Conferences.* This technique is particularly useful for those parents who do not normally come to school functions. The telephone gives them an opportunity to express their views and helps ensure that a true cross-section of the community is represented in the needs assessment phase. A disadvantage is the amount of time needed to contact large numbers of parents.

4. *Brainstorming Sessions.* Brainstorming allows a free flow of ideas, comments, and suggestions. As a group activity, the emphasis should be on *quantity* of ideas rather than on *quality*. Any idea should be accepted and recorded for all to see. These sessions may be initiated by asking parents to respond to an open-ended statement such as "I could help my child in reading more, if I...." This technique can often generate a wide range of responses.

5. *Informal Interviews.* The value of informal, face-to-face contacts with parents outside of school should not be underestimated. The shopping mall, hardware store, or doctor's office can provide excellent opportunities for talking with parents informally about a parent program. Their offhand comments, obtained in a relaxed and nonthreatening environment, can often be especially useful in preparing questionnaires, checklists, and other formal needs assessment instruments.

Some methods of needs assessment are more appropriate for certain groups or educational situations than others. Also, some assessment techniques are more appropriately administered by certain individuals within the school than others. Training, time, contact opportunities, or cost may preclude some school personnel from engaging in some parts of the needs assessment phase. Regardless, it is important that formal and informal methods be used to complement each other and that they be chosen and sequenced according to the group being surveyed and the personnel available to administer them.

The Needs Assessment Strategies figure summarizes some aspects of needs assessment activities and categorizes them according to their applicability for school personnel. These classifications are not finite, but simply suggest that by carefully portioning assessment responsibilities among several individuals or groups, the effectiveness of needs assessment can be increased.

Following the summary of needs assessment strategies are examples of five formal methods. They are offered as samples of self-designed instruments that may be useful in certain situations. Readers are encouraged to adapt these or construct their own in order to fit different groups and educational settings. Only by using a variety of specifically designed assessment tools can educators ensure that the needs of parents are being fairly and accurately addressed in a reading program. And only by involving in program planning all principal parties (administrators, classroom teachers, reading specialists, as well as parents) can the broad base of support critical for a program's success be generated.

Needs Assessment Strategies	Classroom Teachers	Reading Specialists	Administrators
Formal			
Standardized Tests		X	X
Do not reflect values of parents, but may indicate need for parental intervention to alleviate student deficiencies.			
Questionnaires	X	X	X
Can be used at any time to survey interests. Drawback is that not all parents want to reply.			
Attitude Scales	X	X	
Appropriate to determine affective needs.			
Surveys		X	X
Advantage is that all members can provide input into development of programs.			
Interest Inventories	X		
Can provide useful data for smaller groups.			
Self-Evaluative Scales	X		
Provide useful information on personal level.			
Informal			
Individual Conferences	X		
Useful in assessing personal needs.			
Small Group Discussions	X	X	X
Allow for interaction between members; need leader for proper direction.			
Telephone Conferences	X	X	X
Provide input for parents unable to come to school, but could be time consuming.			
Parent Meetings	X	X	X
Need for informality to keep discussion going.			
Informal Interviews	X	X	
Important for face-to-face contact.			
Brainstorming Sessions	X	X	
Allow for free flow of ideas, reactions, etc.			

Fredericks and Taylor

Guidelines for Needs Assessment

An assessment of needs should:

1. Be the first step in developing a parent program in reading based on what parents really desire, not what can be easily implemented (Lyons et al., 1981).
2. Use a variety of formal and informal devices and do not rely on traditional, formal questionnaires.
3. Determine the desires of both active and inactive parents so that a wide range of opinions is sampled.
4. Involve parents in designing and carrying out strategies of needs assessment.
5. Continue throughout a program to give parents sufficient opportunity to tell what they want.

Parent Questionnaire

Please look at the statements below. Following the statements are three boxes labeled First, Second, and Third Choice. Indicate your choices by writing in the number of each statement that you choose.

I would like to have more information on:
1. Reading aloud to my child.
2. Reading games I can make.
3. How reading is taught in the schools.
4. How I can test my child in reading.
5. Reading and television.
6. How to develop a home library.
7. How to develop good attitudes toward reading.
8. What to listen for when my child reads to me.
9. How to build my child's vocabulary.
10. Selecting books and magazines for my child.
11. Motivating my child to read.
12. How to develop good comprehension skills.
13. Reading and health (vision, hearing, etc.)
14. How to improve my child's phonics skills.
15. How children learn to read.
16. Homework and reading.
17. Selecting good books.
18. _____ .

First Choice ☐   *My Child(ren) is/are in grade(s)*

Second Choice ☐   (Please Circle)

Third Choice ☐   K   1   2   3   4   5   6

Parent Attitude Survey

Please put an "x" in the box after each statement that best expresses your feelings.

    A means I strongly agree
    B means I agree
    C means I am undecided
    D means I disagree
    E means I strongly disagree

	A	B	C	D	E
1. My child enjoys reading at home					
2. Reading to children is important					
3. I am satisfied with my child's reading progress					
4. I enjoy reading in my free time					
5. Reading is the most important subject in school					
6. Parents should help their children learn					
7. Playing reading games can help children learn					
8. Children should know how to read fast					
9. Knowing all the words is important in reading					
10. All students should have a library card					
11. Television is bad					
12. Books and magazines are valuable reading materials					
13. Good vision is important for good reading					
14. Most teachers can't teach reading very well					
15. Families should read more together					

Fredericks and Taylor

Please finish the following incomplete sentences.

1. Reading can be

2. I enjoy reading

3. When I read to my child

4. Some children's books are

5. My child's teacher doesn't

6. My child's reading level is

7. Comprehension is

8. Most parent workshops are

9. I could help my child in reading if

10. The reading specialist should

Parent Checklist

Check the option which best describes your child's reading performance.

	very good	good	fair	poor	don't know
1. Phonics skills	___	___	___	___	___
2. Vocabulary	___	___	___	___	___
3. Comprehension	___	___	___	___	___
4. Silent reading	___	___	___	___	___
5. Oral reading	___	___	___	___	___
6. Motivation	___	___	___	___	___
7. Attitude	___	___	___	___	___

Check the option which best describes the kinds of information or projects the school makes available to parents.

	very good	good	fair	poor	don't know
1. School newsletter	___	___	___	___	___
2. Parent workshops	___	___	___	___	___
3. TV programs	___	___	___	___	___
4. Radio spots	___	___	___	___	___

5. Parent pamphlet   ___   ___   ___   ___   ___
6. Family Nights   ___   ___   ___   ___   ___
7. Teacher conferences   ___   ___   ___   ___   ___

Interest Survey

Below is a list of programs, topics, or ideas to help parents become involved in their child's education. It is our intent with this survey to provide you with meaningful programs, based on *your* needs, that might contribute to the success of our school. Please record your degree of interest by marking the appropriate space after each statement.

I would like to become involved in my child's education or in his/her school in the following ways:

	Much Interest	Some Interest	No Interest
1. Receive monthly newsletters of reading and math tips for me to share with my child at home.	___	___	___
2. Volunteer a certain number of hours each week to work as a teacher's aide in a classroom.	___	___	___
3. Attend a parent course to find out how I can help my child learn better.	___	___	___
4. Visit a *Home Help Center* set up in the school where I could borrow materials, games, puzzles, and other activities that my child and I could work on at home.	___	___	___
5. Become involved as a "Teaching Paraprofessional" to make visits to other parents at home to work on learning activities for their children.	___	___	___
6. Receive visits from a "Teaching Paraprofessional" to work on learning activities for my children.	___	___	___

Fredericks and Taylor

7. Attend a schoolwide educational conference for parents. The conference would have various workshops, sessions, and presentations by several speakers on many different topics. _____ _____ _____

8. Receive a booklet of information on tips and suggestions that I could use to help my child in reading and math. _____ _____ _____

9. Attend a workshop to make learning games to boost math and reading skills for my child to use at home. _____ _____ _____

10. Have more conferences with my child's teacher. _____ _____ _____

11. Visit the school to see how reading and math are taught in the classroom. _____ _____ _____

12. Visit a class to share my job or hobby with the students. _____ _____ _____

13. Help make and construct activities and materials for use in classrooms. _____ _____ _____

14. Attend a miniworkshop where various teachers would present parent programs. _____ _____ _____

15. Enroll in an adult education course on how to become an effective parent. _____ _____ _____

16. Read to groups of children in school. _____ _____ _____

17. Work with other parents in the school to help teachers as needed. _____ _____ _____

18. Learn about specific books I can get to help me help my child at home. _____ _____ _____

19. Become a member of a school advisory council to discuss with teachers ways to improve the school's academic programs. _____ _____ _____

20. Tutor youngsters who are having difficulties in reading or math. _____ _____ _____

Self-Evaluative Scale

Please check (✓) those items that you or your child do at home. Place two checks (✓✓) in front of those items that are done every day. Leave blank those items that are not done.

_____ 1. I read with my child every day.

_____ 2. I watch and talk about TV with my child.

_____ 3. My child reads many different kinds of materials.

_____ 4. My child has his/her own library or bookcase.

_____ 5. I talk with my child about school.

_____ 6. I enjoy reading a wide variety of materials.

_____ 7. I help my child select his/her reading material.

_____ 8. I write down stories my child tells me.

_____ 9. My child has many experiences outside our home.

_____ 10. I encourage my child in reading.

_____ 11. I give my child books for birthdays or other occasions.

_____ 12. I talk over the things my child reads.

_____ 13. I attend parent conferences at school.

_____ 14. Our family visits the local public library.

_____ 15. Our family plays word games.

_____ 16. My child has time to read at home.

_____ 17. I help my child with his/her homework.

_____ 18. I enjoy reading in my free time.

_____ 19. I ask my child questions about his/her books.

Phase 2: Planning

While needs assessment is the first step in developing a parent program, the information gathered must now be analyzed and shaped into goals of the program. In the phase of planning, the activities that will lead the program to those goals are chosen and sequenced.

It is crucial to the success of a parent program that an organized and efficient plan of action come out of the planning process. Often, parent programs are developed merely to add a kind of window dressing to a school's educational effort or to satisfy the demands of a few individuals. However, successful programs come about through comprehensive and specific planning that addresses a few well-documented needs of the educational community. Program planning also allows time for a consensus to be reached by administrators, teachers, and parents. This consensus in turn generates the awareness and support of the program that are necessary for its success. Indeed, systematic planning which includes all participants has proven to be the most effective way to meet the needs and achieve the goals of parent programs (Gardner & O'Loughlin-Snyder, 1981). These goals form the answer to the central question for all parent programs: What will parents learn and how will their children profit?

Specifically, a program goal is an ongoing purpose that provides a sense of direction over a certain length of time. It describes a measurable, desired result to be accomplished within that time period. These objectives, usually stated in behavioral terms, include what program participants should know or be able to do at the conclusion of the parent project in reading. Therefore, the program planning phase of necessity requires the identification of performance objectives based on identified needs. These behavioral objectives are also important for two other reasons: they encourage the development of appropriate activities to achieve specific goals; and they allow for a systematic, empirical evaluation of the total program.

The following questions are offered as guidelines for developing objectives for parent programs. If the objectives are adequately concrete and realistic, then a program planner should be able to answer these questions specifically and positively.

1. What are the means by which the objectives will be achieved?
2. How are parents involved in accomplishing these objectives?
3. Will all participants succeed equally?
4. Are the objectives based upon the desires of the participants?
5. Are the objectives so involved that failure is inevitable?
6. Are the activities of the program consistent with the objectives?
7. Are all group members involved in a forward direction?
8. How will it be known if the objectives have been achieved?
9. What will things be like when the objectives have been accomplished?

Program planning should be an organized process, whether for parent involvement in reading or any other academic project. The following sequence offers a design for individuals and committees to follow in planning a purposeful program.

Determine a few areas of greatest need. Data from the needs assessment should be carefully analyzed to determine trends, strengths and weaknesses, and the interests of the people surveyed. A few of the strongest needs should be selected for development into needs statements.

Give priority to certain needs. Since all the needs identified in an assessment cannot be sufficiently addressed in a single program, what merits immediate and strong attention should be selected and addressed.

Analyze the selected needs. It is important to determine what a specific problem is, who is affected, and what caused it. Addressing a clearly understood and well-defined need increases the likelihood of a successful program.

Project a long range plan. The most effective programs extend over a specified period of time (Henderson, 1981). "One shot" projects are difficult to integrate into the curriculum and may have little effect on student achievement. Long range planning, on the other hand, considers the feasibility of the project, the available resources, and any existing constraints.

Brainstorm for action. Brainstorming should be done as a group and without necessarily regarding the quality of ideas. Brainstorming with parents, teachers and administrators allows different "voices" to contribute for the good of the whole.

Outline a plan of action. The ideas generated through brainstorming should provide several possible designs for the parent program. The planning committee must select only those ideas that fit within the constraints brought on by time, money, and facilities.

Develop details for the plan of action. Identifying the specifics of any planned program in reading also means delegating the responsibility for them among both teachers and parents. In addition, the planning committee should consider what resources will be required and how the activities will be evaluated.

Develop a timeline. It is important that all community members participate in the development of an appropriate timeline. Since social, personal, and educational considerations may affect the course of the planned program, target dates and times should be determined through a consensus of opinion.

The following planning example is offered as an illustration of the dynamics of program planning. It presents the results of one school's needs assessment and the planning steps that were undertaken to develop an adult education course in the East Penn, Pennsylvania, School District. The program was eventually entitled "Helping Your Child to Read" and was carried out in 1980-1981.

Planning Example

"Helping Your Child to Read"
East Penn School District, 1980
Emmaus, Pennsylvania

Determine Areas of Greatest Need

How to help with comprehension.

How to build positive attitudes toward reading.

What is involved in the reading process?

Prioritize Needs
What is involved in the reading process?
Analyze Top Priority Need
Parents have misconceptions about what is involved in the reading process and about how they can help their children.
Project a Long Range Plan

Fall, first year	Disseminate IRA publications
Spring, first year	Parent training workshops
Summer, second year	Summer Activities Handbook
Fall, third year	Adult education course

Brainstorm for Action Alternatives
Family Reading Fair
Visitation week
Individual parent conferences
Role modeling
Parent training workshops
Adult education course
Develop a Plan of Action
Adult education course, "Helping Your Child to Read"
Minireading fair
Develop Details for Plan of Action
Submit course proposal
Communicate with administrative contact person
Develop tentative course outline
Delegate specific sessions to staff members
Develop class session format
Refine course outline after assessing needs/interests of course participants
Document—develop mid/end point evaluation instruments
Develop a Timeline
Define logical sequence for topic presentation within course time frame

Guidelines for Program Planning
Program planning should:
1. Involve both educators and parents and thus lead them to share a mutual commitment to the program.
2. Be based on only a few, clearly defined needs.
3. Develop specific and long range goals that will provide direction for the program.

4. Select appropriate activities, from a multitude of suggestions, that will lead to achieving the program's goals.

5. Offer participants several degrees of involvement so that the program can be flexible and adaptable to the exigencies of people and their resources.

Phase 3: Implementation

The previous two stages concerned the importance of needs assessment and the value of program planning based upon the results of the assessment. This section presents guidelines for implementation—actually beginning and carrying out step-by-step a parent program in reading. For the most part, the process of implementation involves coordinating the two elements of personnel tasks and time to bring about the desired program, a coordination that is as essential to parent program as it is to any educational endeavor.

The purpose of this discussion is twofold: 1) to provide an understanding of individual roles and their responsibilities, and 2) to emphasize the proper scheduling of program activities so that a majority of parents have the opportunity to participate in at least one portion of the project (Lyons et al.,1981). There are two key questions that must be answered satisfactorily during this phase of a parent program: What should be the specific responsibilities of those involved? What are the criteria for scheduling activities that will allow a modern family to be involved in the program?

Roles and Responsibilities

A parent program in reading, like so many projects, can be only as good as the people involved in it. Success has to be built upon a clear delineation of their roles and on their cooperation with each other. Also, a parent program has its best chance of success when it involves a variety of people—administrators, classroom teachers, individual parents, parent groups—and thus acquires a firm and broad foundation of support.

Below are some of the questions that should be considered by each person holding a particular position and also by the person or group responsible for implementing the program. Although job titles and positions may vary among different school districts, these questions, as well as the input and support they can elicit, are important for a smooth running and effective program.

School Board

1. Do the members of the school board support and encourage the development of a parent program in reading?

2. Can school board members provide funds for beginning and carrying out a parent program?

3. Are school board members willing to help promote the program?

Superintendent

1. Is the superintendent aware of the potential impact of a parent program in reading?

2. Will the superintendent provide support by giving released time for staff, and by providing funding and facilities?

3. Is the superintendent prepared to act as a knowledgeable and active link in the implementation process?

Administrative Staff

1. Are administrators knowledgeable in the areas of parent involvement and reading instruction?

2. Are administrators aware of the methods and materials that will be used in the parent project?

3. Are administrators willing to develop their expertise in parent involvement as well as communicate their support throughout the local community?

Building Principal

1. Since school reading programs are often a reflection of the school leader, has the principal established parent involvement as a priority for the reading program?

2. Does the principal encourage and support the efforts of the staff in developing active programs?

3. Does the principal demonstrate an active interest in parent involvement in children's reading?

4. Will principals use the channels of communication available to them in order to promote enthusiasm and interest in a program?

Parents

1. Are parents aware of the advantages of their participation in a parent project in reading?

2. Will parents be recruited for different stages of program development?

3. Will the voices of parents be given equal weight in all decisions so that they will feel an essential part of the reading program?

Reading Consultant

1. Is the reading consultant prepared to attend to all of the details associated with a parent program, sometimes taking the leadership role and sometimes willing to stand in the shadows?

2. Is the reading consultant prepared to make a public relations effort so that members of the school community are informed of the progress of the program?

3. Can the reading consultant assume the duties of a resource person, providing groups and individuals with research data, information, ideas, materials, expertise and energy?

Classroom Teachers

1. Are teachers aware of the effect of parent involvement on their students' reading achievement, and are they prepared to devote the extra effort needed to include parents on the reading team?

2. Are teachers willing to make additional preparations in order to ensure active participation on the part of parents?

3. Will teachers provide materials, schedule conferences, make phone calls, and assume other duties in order to promote a parent program in reading?

Using the talents and resources of many people establishes a necessary foundation upon which implementation can be based. Viewed as a pyramid, this collection of groups and individuals can offer firm support for a variety of reading programs, each designed to offer parents an active role in the reading development of their children.

Scheduling

There are three obvious requirements for an adequate schedule. First, it should contain a timeline that will allow for the unhurried and full completion of all planned activites. A good schedule should also anticipate and be prepared to accommodate other events, both expected and unexpected, that may affect the participation of parents. Sports events, community activities, season of the year and the weather it brings all must be considered when planning activities. Finally, good scheduling anticipates changes that may occur in the middle of a program. Flagging interests, newly identified needs, and the loss of leaders also may affect a program and require important midcourse adjustments.

Two more guidelines for scheduling focus on the main participants and their needs. First, parents should be recruited for all stages of the program, and their participation should be scheduled to fit their personal schedules as closely as possible. Simply stated, scheduling should be for the needs of parents, not the convenience of educators (Lyons et al., 1981). Second, the reactions of all participants (especially parents and teachers) need to be carefully monitored and reacted to in schedules that change dynamically as the program unfolds. A schedule carved in stone at the beginning of a program can become a heavy burden once real people with their real needs become involved.

Many parent programs are multidimensional in nature. They offer a variety of activities that are designed to meet several different needs. It is important, however, that the separate parts of a program do not overtake or grow larger than the umbrella project itself. They must remain integrated in a program that moves coherently and surely towards its stated goals. To keep the varied activities focused on the overall objectives of the program, their design and scheduling should be built around four key concerns:

Awareness

1. What activities or contact procedures will bring the program to the attention of a majority of parents and students?

2. How will teachers be adequately informed of the program?

Motivation

1. How will parents and students be encouraged to participate in the scheduled program and maintain their interest over an extended period of time?

2. How will teachers participate in the activities?

Involvement

1. How will participants and students be made more aware of their responsibilities in terms of the requirements of the program? What activities will insure that they stay active?

2. What activities will teachers use to encourage involvement?

Recognition

1. Have ongoing, interim, and terminal methods of reward and recognition been built into the program for both parents and students?

2. How will teachers be recognized? Will teachers be responsible for giving rewards and recognition?

The chart on p. 20 illustrates how the various activities of a program can be scheduled to generate the four essential ingredients for program success: awareness, motivation, involvement, and recognition. The activities for each of the areas have been divided according to their applicability to either parents or teachers. This division reflects the scheduling parameters of this particular program ("Parents as Reading Partners" in the Catasauqua, Pennsylvania, Area School District), and also how all participants in a program have the same need to be aware of the program, motivated and involved in it, and recognized for their contributions. Most of the materials that accompany the activities in the "Parents as Reading Partners" program can be found in the appendix. Readers are encouraged to excerpt these for actual use or as models for implementation activities that bring parents and teachers together, stimulate them to stay involved, and reward their efforts to help children be better readers.

Program Title: "Parents As Reading Partners"

Objective: Parents Will Read with their Child for 15 Minutes Each Day for a Minimum of 20 Days Each Month

	AWARENESS	MOTIVATION	INVOLVEMENT	RECOGNITION
PARENT	• PTA or Parent Advisory Council • Newsletters • Open House • Newspaper articles • Radio, TV spots • Letter from child • Letters from principal, superintendent • Meetings • Pamphlets • Posters • Letters from other parents	• Newsletters for sharing • Book lists • Ongoing display • Book Fair • Family certificates • Schoolwide spirit contest • Involve local writer • Tour of newspaper • Drawings • Parent buttons • Noncompetitive recordkeeping system • Photos of families reading together	• Parent conferences • Monthly meetings at school • Recordkeeping at school • Book swap in library • Posters for local stores • Monthly calendars given to each family to record times and dates read	• Certificates • "Reading Family of the Month" • "Weekly Reader" display board • Buttons • Awards, prizes • Special parent night • Assembly • Parent picnic • Letter from superintendent, principal, mayor • Book donations
TEACHER	• Beginning of year inservice program • Information packet • Teacher newsletter • Slide presentation • Handouts • Bibliographies • Presentation by another district • Faculty meeting	• Certificate for teachers having most participation in classroom • Monthly award for teacher • Button awards • Administrative pressure • Swap day between classes • Paperback book exchange • Encouragement from principal • Signs/posters	• Selections of books to be sent home • Swap shop • Parent contact • Open House • Letters • Phone calls • Daily reading time with class • Classroom newsletters • Hall murals • Assembly program • Monthly award • PTA/PTO	• Badges, books, gifts, prizes from local merchants • Classroom sharing by pupils • Use PA system • Teacher recognition when child makes progress • Newspapers, radio, TV • Yearly prize • Picnic • Party • District newsletter • Awards night • Bulletin board display

Fredericks and Taylor

Other Factors in Implementation

The preceding discussion has focused on defining the individual roles and responsibilities of participants and on drawing up a sound schedule for the activities that will make others aware of the program and involved in it. While delegating responsibility and scheduling activities form the basis for implementation, attention must also be given to the nuts and bolts concerns of bringing a program to life. Strategies must be mapped, and available resources accessed.

The following chart illustrates the concerns that need attention and suggests sample strategies for dealing with them. The list of strategies is not intended to be exhaustive. Local conditions may prevent the use of some, while others not listed may be of more importance to a given program. For example, small rural schools may not have access to community buildings or social agencies that could be used by programs in an urban setting. The larger districts may even have their own public relations person who could take responsibility for selling the program through a steady flow of press releases, radio announcements, and direct mailings to parents. Regardless of how they are addressed, the implementation concerns of parent programs—large or small, simple or complex—are the same. Those who will staff the program must be trained; time for their training must be provided; money to support the program must be acquired; parents must be contacted; and the use of facilities must be secured.

Factors in Implementation

AREAS OF CONCERN	IMPLEMENTATION STRATEGIES
INSERVICE/STAFF DEVELOPMENT	• Research on parent involvement • Outside consultants • Involvement of entire staff • Released time • Meetings, workshops, conferences • Special programs, visitations
TIME	• Substitute teachers, aides • Establishment of time line • Scheduling of activities • Incorporation into classroom process • Redefining staff roles • Modification of school hours

IMPLEMENTATION PHASES	<ul><li>Publicity/promotion</li><li>PREP</li><li>Review current program</li><li>Program follow up</li><li>Class management</li><li>Variety of activities</li><li>Emphasis on total staff involvement</li></ul>
BUDGET	<ul><li>District sources</li><li>PTA</li><li>Local community</li><li>Private foundations</li><li>State department of education</li><li>IRA</li><li>Federal sources</li></ul>
COMMUNICATION/CONTACT	<ul><li>Letters, printed material</li><li>Personal contact</li><li>Meetings/conferences</li><li>Awards/certificate of participation</li><li>Progress reports</li><li>"Telephone tree"</li><li>Volunteers</li></ul>
FACILITIES	<ul><li>Classroom</li><li>Duplication services</li><li>Community agencies/organizations</li><li>Churches, YMCA, etc.</li><li>Parents' homes</li></ul>
PARENT MATERIALS	<ul><li>Keyed to instructional program</li><li>Games</li><li>Family projects</li><li></li><li></li><li></li><li></li></ul>

Guidelines for Program Implementation

When being implemented, a program should:

1. Involve a variety of school personnel as well as parents so that no program becomes the vehicle of one person's desires.

2. Coordinate the responsibilities of individuals so that they work as a team toward a common goal.

3. Have a flexible schedule that is subject to periodic evaluation and to alteration as local conditions and the needs of participants change.

4. Integrate classroom instruction and program activities so that the two reinforce each other.

5. Contain activities and procedures that will create awareness, motivation, and involvement of participants as well as allow for recognition of their contributions and achievements.

6. Take advantage of local conditions and resources.

Phase 4: Evaluation

The choice to evaluate the program is a manifestly logical and necessary one. Thus far needs have been identified, objectives drawn up based on those needs, and activities implemented that are designed to accomplish the program's goals. The next step is to determine if and when those goals have been reached, and to what degree the behavior of the participants has been changed in the desired direction. Making these two determinations in an empirically sound way, so that the truth about a program's effectiveness can be known, is the main purpose of evaluation.

In addition, evaluation is a part of a process that occurs both during and at the end of a program. While a program is actually in progress, information collected formally and informally can provide an immediate indication of whether a program is on the right track or whether changes are needed. At the end of the program, the information from the evaluation becomes the first step in the planning and implementation of the next program, thus providing a place to begin rather than merely end.

For the evaluation to provide reliable information about the objectives and activities of the program, data must be collected systematically and must be comprehensive (Williams et al., 1981). To achieve this goal, several specific guidelines for evaluation are important. First, it can be both interesting and valid to involve parents in designing the questions that will determine what will be measured in the very program of which they have been a part. During a program, parents take on much of the role of educators, acquiring the right and responsibility to help define the parameters of success and failure of their "students." It is common sense that everyone intimately involved in the program should have a voice in its evaluation.

Second, the information must be gathered, analyzed, shared, and put to use either while the program is in progress (in the case of ongoing evaluation), or at its conclusion to encourage reflection upon what has happened and to prepare for the next program. Putting the information to use helps both educators and parents to effect closure, an important mental event in which the activity is perceived as complete and thus can be reflected upon and learned from more easily.

But most of all, for an evaluation to be useful, the information gathered must be as complete and varied as possible. This comprehensiveness is achieved only when a variety of evaluation instruments is used. The following discussion focuses on numerous strategies for evaluation, some formal and some informal, some appropriate for ongoing as well as concluding evaluations, and some that measure the impact of the program on both children and parents.

Formal Methods of Evaluation

1. *Surveys.* These permit responses to a variety of evaluation statements or questions. One of the most important considerations in developing a survey is that it be written in terms of the specific program objectives which were spelled out during the planning phase. Typically, surveys are used as a concluding evaluation instrument since many incorporate a variety of both open-ended and closed questions and statements. One advantage of properly prepared surveys is that they can be developed to evaluate the impact of a program on either parents or their children.

2. *Scales.* Used at the end of the program, scales can measure the impact of a program on parents and changes in the relationship with their child. The information gathered from these instruments can also be valuable in determining a program's worth in terms of affective concerns. Scales can be easily developed for the students whose parents participated in a program.

3. *Response Sheets.* A major consideration in any evaluative process is gathering information about a program's effectiveness during the course of the program. Response sheets provide a straightforward and simple way for participants to express their reactions to different parts of the program as they occur. This information then becomes helpful in planning any changes in program design or format.

4. *Checklists.* Checklists can be used in a variety of situations. Because of their ease of administration and interpretation, checklists are appropriate as summative instruments for either parents or students. Because checklists can be rapidly scored, they are also appropriate as a medial method of evaluation. The informality of checklists offers respondents a rapid means of presenting their views about a program and its impact on their lives.

5. *Written Narratives.* Surveys and checklists are valuable but do not always allow parents to express their views in a personal or extended way. The comments in written narratives, either anonymous or signed, can be beneficial in ongoing

evaluations and in concluding evaluations. However, the possible reaction of parents to written work needs to be assessed before this kind of instrument is used.

Many of the instruments for needs assessment will be appropriate for evaluation also. Data collected during concluding evaluations can be compared with the information from the initial needs assessment to determine shifts in attitudes or skills among the program participants. With this comparison, the effectiveness of a program over a specific period of time can be gauged.

Informal Methods of Evaluation

1. *Discussions.* Conducted in a relaxed and informal atmosphere, discussions can let parents express their views about a program in a nonthreatening format. Appropriate as ongoing evaluation measures, discussions can be made a regular part of the scheduled sessions. They also may be formalized by having a special set of questions prepared beforehand to serve as a springboard for the group.

2. *Open House Visitations.* Many parent programs schedule a series of wrap-up activities at the end of a program. These projects allow educators and parents to share views and information about a program. Their disadvantage is that not all parents have the opportunity to come to the school during open house programs. Thus the information gathered from the process may come mostly from those parents likely to give positive evaluations of a program. A particular advantage is that parents and children often attend together, thus presenting an opportunity for questions to all members of the family.

3. *Observations.* Observing the interaction that takes place between parents and their children can yield valuable information about a program's effectiveness. It should be remembered that observations are being made in a setting that may be different from those in which the parents and children normally interact. Observations must, of course, be validated by other evaluation measures.

4. *Sharing Sessions.* Informal sharing sessions, which can include parents and students, together or alone, can also provide important information. Whether conducted individually or in small groups, these sessions allow people to interact and contribute perceptions about a program's effectiveness.

Evaluation strategies can span many groups and can be appropriate in a variety of situations. It will be necessary, of course, to select those techniques that best match the features of a specific program. Following are several examples of formal evaluative measures. They are presented as samples of instruments that have been used in specific parent programs. Readers may find that with some changes these instruments can be appropriate for their particular program. Only by using a variety of instruments—formal and informal, ongoing and concluding—will it be possible to determine if the program's goals are being met or whether changes are necessary during the course of a program: the two primary functions of evaluation.

Guidelines for Program Evaluation

An evaluation should:

1. Be keyed to the stated objectives of the program.

2. Assess the effect of the program while it is ongoing as well as at its end.

3. Involve parents and students in the design, administration, and analysis of the evaluation strategies.

4. Use a variety of evaluation tools: formal and informal, parent and student impact, ongoing and concluding.

5. Gather information for a purpose: to change an existing program or to plan for a future one.

Home Help Center

Please check (✓) those items in each section which best describe your evaluation of the Home Help Center. Check as many as needed.

1. *Materials*

____ There was a wide variety of materials.

____ The materials were appropriate for my child.

____ My child enjoyed the materials.

____ The materials were too easy.

____ I was not able to obtain enough materials.

____ More materials are needed for certain skills.

2. *Operation*

____ The hours were convenient.

____ The Center should be open more.

____ I had sufficient knowledge of the Center.

____ Personnel were helpful.

____ The check out procedure was easy.

____ It was easy to obtain the materials.

3. *As a Result of Using the Center, My Child*

____ has shown improvement in his/her reading.

____ seems to like reading more.

____ understands that reading is important.

____ can sound out words better.

____ can understand more of what he/she reads.

____ feels more successful in reading.

We are interested in increasing parent participation in the Home Help Center. Please check as many items as necessary to express your preferences.

One check (✓) indicates a preference.

Two checks (✓✓) indicate a stronger preference.

Fredericks and Taylor

4. *I would like to have the following means of communication as part of the Home Help Center*

_____ monthly newsletter.

_____ telephone contacts.

_____ brochures, flyers, and handouts with specific reading tips and suggestions.

_____ monthly meetings with the reading specialist to construct activities and games for my child.

_____ special individual conferences.

_____ parent training sessions.

_____ other (please describe).

5. *I would prefer the Center to be open*

_____ in the morning.

_____ in the afternoon.

_____ in the evening.

_____ on weekends.

_____ in the morning and afternoon.

_____ in the morning, afternoon, and evening.

_____ other (please describe).

6. *In general, the Home Help Center was*

_____ excellent.

_____ good.

_____ ok.

_____ not too bad.

_____ poorly done.

7. Please list any ideas, suggestions, or comments you might have concerning the Sheckler Home Help Center. Your thoughts will be a *major* part of planning next year's program.

_____

Signature (Optional)

Parent Scale

Directors: You and your child have participated in the *Bookworms, Inc.* family reading program this year. We are interested in learning your feelings about our program. Please circle the letter following each statement that describes how you feel about that statement.

My Child

1. understands more of what he/she reads.   A B C D E
2. reads more books now.   A B C D E
3. enjoys reading with family members.   A B C D E
4. likes to go to the library.   A B C D E
5. has a better attitude about reading.   A B C D E
6. can understand more words.   A B C D E
7. feels good about what he/she does.   A B C D E
8. enjoys the *Bookworms, Inc.* Program.   A B C D E
9. reads more on his/her own.   A B C D E
10. would like to get more books.   A B C D E

As a Parent I

11. read with my child on a regular basis.   A B C D E
12. can now help my child in reading.   A B C D E
13. feel good about my child's reading.   A B C D E
14. would like to know more about how I can help.   A B C D E
15. would like to know more about other reading programs.   A B C D E

Family Involvement Workshops

Midpoint Evaluation

Directions: Please respond to each item by circling the number which best describes your reaction to the workshops.

	High				Low	
Purpose clear	5	4	3	2	1	Purpose unclear
Well organized	5	4	3	2	1	Poorly organized
Leader well prepared	5	4	3	2	1	Leader poorly prepared
Content appropriate	5	4	3	2	1	Content inappropriate
Coverage Comprehensive	5	4	3	2	1	Coverage superficial
Materials used helpful	5	4	3	2	1	Materials not helpful

Stimulating activities	5	4	3	2	1	Boring activities
Fast paced	5	4	3	2	1	Slow paced
Discussion adequate	5	4	3	2	1	Discussion inadequate
Relevant to family situation	5	4	3	2	1	Not relevant to family situation
Met my objectives	5	4	3	2	1	Did not meet my objectives

1. What are the strong points of the workshops?

2. What could be improved about the workshops?

3. Additional comments.

Parent Checklist: Family Reading Program

Please check (✓) those items in each section which best describe the changes in your attitudes, behaviors, or skills. Check as many as needed to describe changes in you or your family during the course of this program. This checklist is anonymous; however, you may feel free to use your name, if desired.

1. *Changes in Attitude/Behavior*
   _____ I enjoy working with my child more.
   _____ I enjoy our sharing times together.
   _____ Our family reads more books together.
   _____ Our family chooses reading as a free-time activity.
   _____ We visit the library more.
   _____ We watch less TV.
   _____ Our family shares magazines, newspapers, and books.

2. *Changes in Attitude toward Reading*
   My child
   _____ seems to enjoy reading more.
   _____ enjoys reading with me.
   _____ enjoys reading to other members of the family.
   _____ brings more books home now.
   _____ sees reading as a worthwhile activity.

3. *Personal Changes*

_____ I understand more about the reading process.

_____ I can now help my child succeed.

_____ I have a more positive attitude about school.

_____ I can help my child with his/her homework.

_____ I can make reading a natural part of our family activities.

_____ I can now serve as a good role model for my child.

_____ I understand the importance of reading in my child's life.

Student Survey

1. What did you like most about the "Parents as Reading Partners" program this year?

2. What didn't you like about the program?

3. I thought the program was helpful for me.

_____ yes   _____ no   _____ don't know

4. I like to read.

_____ very much   _____ sometimes   _____ not at all

5. This year my parents and I read

_____ more than 20 books _____ 10 to 20 books   _____ 5 to 10 books

6. I like to read in my spare time.

_____ always   _____ sometimes   _____ never

7. I think that parents and children should read together more.

_____ yes   _____ no   _____ don't know

8. I think that I can be a better reader.

_____ yes   _____ no   _____ don't know

9. I plan on doing some reading this summer.

_____ yes   _____ no   _____ maybe

10. What would you like to see in the "Parents as Reading Partners" program for next year?

Questions for Evaluation Discussion

1. Have you noticed any changes in your child's attitude toward reading this year?

2. What were the most satisfying parts of the program for you?

3. What parts of the program do you feel were the weakest?

4. Would your family like to continue in the program next year? Why?

5. In what areas of reading would you like to help your child most?

6. What ideas can you offer to improve the program for next year?

7. Any additional comments or suggestions?

Model Program: "Parents as Reading Partners"

Phase One: Needs Assessment

Following a meeting at a local university on the value of parents and children reading together, a group of educators and parents from a nearby elementary school began an assessment of needs to determine if a parent reading program should be developed. The reading specialist took the responsibility for talking with parents individually during spring parent-teacher conferences. He also conducted a poll of students participating in the district's Chapter I reading program.

A locally constructed questionnaire was sent to a random sample of parents prior to the end of the school year. Based upon the information gathered with these three measures, several needs statements emerged. It seemed as though parents were not reading regularly with their children at home, although they realized the importance of this family activity. Parents indicated a desire to become more active in the reading development of their children. As a result of this assessment, it was felt that a parent-child reading program should be started during the following school year.

The home based program entitled "Parents as Reading Partners" was initiated in the fall. The needs assessment process continued (in the form of phone interviews and a parent survey) to determine if the identified needs were still valid and to locate any potential weaknesses. This part of the needs assessment phase was conducted at the beginning of the school year as well as in the middle. It indicated that the program was well received and participation was widespread. No major alterations in its structure or timeline were needed.

The results of this initial needs assessment phase, as well as subsequent phases, are summarized in the Profile sheet at the end of the discussion of the model program.

Phase Two: Planning

After completing the initial needs assessment, a planning committee of teachers, parents, and the school's reading specialist met to determine the appropriate direction for a parent program in reading. After analyzing the data, they concluded that the greatest need was for parents and students to read together. Because large numbers of parents were not reading with their children on a regular basis, the committee decided that a year long program emphasizing family reading time could best meet the identified need.

The following objective was developed: "Parents will read with children for fifteen minutes each day for twenty days each month." To accomplish this objective, the committee decided that the program should involve the whole school, be based in the home to ensure a minimum of teacher paperwork, and provide periodic reminders to families.

The program was structured in such a way that it would fit into most families' available time. The planning committee felt that a number of periodic awards, certificates, and ceremonies would help sustain interest and desire. The reading specialist would be responsible for maintaining this phase of the program, while parents would be responsible for updating the monthly calendars.

Phase Three: Implementation

After the planning phases, the program committee began to implement the program. First, the roles and responsibilities of those who were directly involved in the program were outlined. The principal, reading specialist, parents, librarian, classroom teachers, students, and community groups were made aware of their part in the program. Next, each of these factors in implementation was addressed.

• Inservice/staff development: Teachers were provided with support materials culled from recent research.

• Time: The program was scheduled to require a minimum of teacher time and to emphasize family time.

• Implementation phases: The reading specialist publicized the program by maintaining contact with the local media.

- Communication/contact: A continuous flow of letters and brochures wa generated throughout the school year.
- Budget: The local Home and School Association provided funds for the printing of calendars and awards.
- Facilities: The program was based in family homes; materials were duplicated in school.
- Parent materials: These were kept to a minimum to provide for a maximum of enjoyment.

The ideas for activities and materials were categorized into the four scheduling classifications and spaced out over the entire program. The following is a partial list: For *Awareness* there were newsletters, pamphlets, "Meet the Teacher" evenings, and flyers. For *Motivation* there were a book fair, a "Family Reading Fair," a record system of the books read by all the families, and family certificates. Monthly calendars, parent-teacher conferences, meetings for those participating, and posters stimulated *Involvement*. Finally, *Recognition* awards included "Weekly Reader" subscriptions, reading buttons, and extra books.

Phase Four: Evaluation

In the evaluation phase of "Parents as Reading Partners," several methods and instruments were part of the program's design. Throughout the year, records were maintained on the number of books read by parents and students at home. In addition, the classroom teachers collected and kept track of the monthly calendars completed by individual students. The reading specialist recorded and monitored the distribution of yearly certificates for the entire school.

There were two concluding instruments. First was a survey distributed to all parents, both those who actively participated and those who did not. Second, a questionnaire was distributed to a random sample of students in all grades (an oral form was used for those in grades K-2).

Additionally, an evaluation was made of standardized test scores. Results from the previous year, in which the program did not exist, were compared with those scores obtained at the conclusion of the project year. All other things considered equal, the overall reading achievement demonstrated a positive gain, attributed in large measure to the "Parents as Reading Partners" program.

On the basis of this evaluation, it was found that both parents and students gained great pleasure from their reading time together. Students whose parents actively participated in the program indicated an increased interest in reading. Finally, a consensus was reached by those involved in the program's design that the project should be continued in future years.

Parent Reading Engagement Profile (PREP)

"Parents As Reading Partners"
Sheckler Elementary School, Catasauqua, Pennsylvania

I. NEEDS ASSESSMENT

Type	Date
Individual	5/81
Student poll	6/81
Questionnaire	6/81
Phone survey	9/81
Parent survey	1/82

Needs Statements

1. Parents are not reading with their children at home.

2. Parents would like to become more involved in their children's reading development.

3. Parents would like to help children enjoy reading more.

II. PROGRAM PLANNING

A. Goals and Objectives
   1. To increase the amount of time children and parents read together this year.
      a. Parents will read with children for 15 min. each day for 20 days each month.

B. Proposed Activities
   1. Initiate PARP program
   2. Keep home-based
   3. Involve whole school
   4. Provide periodic reminders

C. Time Line
   1. Program to run through year
   2. Monthly awards
   3. Yearly certificates
   4. Year-end ceremony

III. PROGRAM IMPLEMENTATION

Responsibilities:
   Principal – letter to parents
   Reading specialist – monitor program
   Parents – total involvement
   Librarians – check out extra books
   Teachers – maintain interest
   Students – certificates and awards

Awareness	Motivation
Newsletters	Book fair
Pamphlets	Family
"Meet the	Reading
Teacher"	Fair
flyers	Record
	system
	Family cert.

Involvement	Recognition
Monthly	Awards
calendars	"Weekly
Conferences	Reader"
Meetings	Buttons
Posters	Extra
	books

IV. EVALUATION

Formal	Informal
Reading tests	Interviews
Parent survey	Observation
Questionnaire	Books read

Evaluation Statements

1. Parents and students enjoyed reading together more.

2. Interest in reading increased.

3. Significant improvement in overall test scores.

4. Program should be continued.

Fredericks and Taylor

4. Whatever form the promotional efforts take, it is important to convey one message to parents: Their involvement will ultimately benefit their children. Parents must believe that their participation in a program will be rewarded by increases in the reading achievement of their youngsters. Thus, when a program's merits are touted, as indeed they should be, the focus must be on the benefit to students.

5. A successful promotional campaign should emphasize the role the entire family plays in a child's academic growth, especially reading skills and attitudes. Some parent programs in reading have, perhaps unconsciously, separated parents and pupils, focusing instead on the training of parents to do certain tasks (Cruz et al., 1981). A different approach would be to focus on the family unit and the influence of each member on the others. Promotion should indicate how students will be involved in the program and thus should be addressed to them as well as to their parents.

In sum, publicity and promotion can increase a program's base of support and also make parents feel they are participating in something fun and important to their children's schooling. People are naturally drawn to popular activities, so public relations work can have a snowball effect. The more parents are excited about and involved in the program, the more others will want to be, too. Accomplishing these objectives requires using a variety of strategies and materials, which can be divided into the categories of either print or nonprint media.

Print Media

According to several estimates, the average American encounters more than four hundred commercial messages each day, many of them in written form. From box tops to emblems on jeans, book covers to billboards, the voices trying to sell something are many. As a result, the competition for a parent's attention is fierce, and only the most effective attempts to communicate through writing can break through the screen used as protection from commercials demanding to be heard. It is important to beware of this competition and to shape promotional materials accordingly.

One characteristic of effective written material concerns its informational content. The ideas and facts offered should be specific, briefly stated, and pitched to the interests of the audience, perhaps containing a personal appeal that is sometimes called a "hook." A lead such as "Reach for the World: Parents and Children Reading Together" bears marked resemblances to an ad for a vacation spot that opens with "Come to Canada: The Endless Surprise." Both summarize the key attraction in a brief and succinct way that also evokes a personal reaction. As a result, both also serve to bring the audience into the piece and provide a reason to read further.

Fredericks and Taylor

Chapter Two

Publicizing and Promoting Parent Programs

There is one plain fact about even the most effective parent program—one that serves the needs of parents, is filled with exciting and innovative activities, and becomes an important part of the reading program. The fact is, if people do not know about it, they cannot profit from it (Farlow, 1979). Telling would-be participants about the program, as well as getting and keeping them involved in it, are the purposes of publicity and promotion. What follows is a discussion of several guidelines for getting the word out and the people in to stay.

Considerations for Publicity and Promotion

1. Programs succeed in large part because parents have been continually presented with an array of information throughout the duration of the project. One shot publicity campaigns are usually ineffectual because there is no follow up that builds upon and sustains an initial interest (Farlow, 1979).

2. As many parts of the school community as possible should be addressed in a promotional campaign. School board members, teachers and community groups or agencies are targets for publicity. Generating a broad base of support is important to the success of a program, and promotional work that reaches many different groups can make them feel they have a stake in the program.

3. In order to fix a program in people's minds, it is helpful to develop a theme ("Reading is a Family Affair"), a title ("Family Reading Fair"), acronym ("Parents as Reading Partners - PARP") or symbol that is easily remembered (Ervin, 1982). Displaying and promoting these attention getters makes the program familiar and reinforces its vitality. Psychologically, people need to see or hear a slogan or symbol a minimum of three times before an association with it becomes automatic and can be acted upon.

A second characteristic is that the language should be highly specific and compact. Most of all, it must be easily understood and, therefore, free of jargon. Consciously lowering the readability level of a letter or brochure for parents may seem cynical, but in truth simply reflects the reality of the communicative situation: a complex, hurried world in which parents are bombarded by competing messages usually attended to for only a matter of seconds. Rarely will parents spend much time on written messages that are not simple, direct, and specific. As an example, here is the opening paragraph from a brochure that was the initial contact with parents in the "Parents as Reading Partners" program:

> I invite you to join our new "Parents as Reading Partners" program. It's a great way to help your child learn *Good Reading Habits.* And it's so easy to participate – there's no money to spend and there are no trips to take. All you have to do is spend 15 minutes each day reading with your child.

The paragraph is written on approximately the fifth grade level and thus can communicate its information effectively even when given a quick reading. It contains specific details in language that is lively and conversational without being condescending. Its underlying message to parents is clear and concrete: this program will be fun, important, and easy for your and your child. Finally, it makes parents want to know more and to continue reading.

A last characteristic is specific to promotional materials for parent programs in reading: Students should be involved in designing, illustrating, writing, and especially in distributing some of the materials to parents. Doing so provides purposeful learning activities as well as builds students' anticipation of the program and involvement in it. Parents also sometimes pay more attention to something their child helped to create than to another form letter from school.

Examples:

• *Letters.* Parents, mayors, chamber of commerce members, community action groups, service organizations, fraternal groups and school board officials are all potential targets for letters announcing a parent program. They should learn of the value and viability of a proposed program and their support and involvement should be solicited.

• *Newspapers.* Aside from the front page and the sports section, the most widely read section of the daily newspaper is letters to the editor. A well crafted, positive letter can be a powerful means for informing the public about the beginning of a program and about how they can contribute to its growth and success. Also, many newspapers have an Op-Ed section which provides citizens with a chance to express their views on a particular issue or concern. This forum offers an excellent opportunity to discuss parent involvement and the value of a specific program at greater length than in a letter. Finally, periodic news releases to the local paper can highlight efforts of local educators and parent groups in the development of a parent project.

• *Guides.* Many schools inform parents and keep them informed about a parent program through the use of several types of guides. Brochures, leaflets, newsletters, booklets, information sheets, and monthly notes have been and continue to be a source of information about the specifics of a parent program. Their value often lies in how well they are designed. The use of graphics, a concise and proper layout, the use of large amounts of "white space," and student input all increase the effect these sources will have. Talking with local advertising agencies may provide tips for writing and designing these pieces.

• *Signs.* One method of keeping the public informed of a parent program is through the use of signs or posters. Distributed throughout the school, in the windows of local businesses and stores, or even in bus and train stations, posters and signs can inform the public about a program.

• *Home Materials.* Schools often send home a variety of materials, homework assignments, or notices to parents on a regular basis. Included with these messages can be a variety of special reports, enclosures or letters directed toward parents. If a familiar logo or symbol is used, parents will be able to recognize the information rapidly and be able to act on it. Special inserts with report cards are one way to get immediate attention from parents, too.

Nonprint Media

It is difficult to ignore the fact that people today receive most of their information through the nonprint media of mass communications. The potential of local media can and should be tapped for publicizing a parent program.

Examples:

• *Public Service Announcements.* Local radio and television stations often like to receive public service announcements about an upcoming project, the efforts of a local organizing committee, or a special event at a school site. Although the format for PSAs is fairly standardized, the twenty to thirty second time limit does offer an excellent and cost effective way to promote a program.

• *Displays and Exhibits.* Local businesses, the post office, or the bank often allow specially designed displays that advertise a particular parent event or program. These displays can be especially effective in areas such as store fronts in the business district.

• *Video.* Many communities have a public television or cable television station that can be used to publicize a program. Television programs developed within the school (if short and to the point) may be appropriate for airing within the service area. Perhaps a local talk show would be interested in interviewing several leaders of a parent project.

• *Face-to-Face Contacts.* One of the most effective selling methods is personal contact with potential clients. In fact, word of mouth is probably as effective and engenders as much credibility as any other promotional effort. Personal contacts, either in person or over the phone, can be effective in informing people about the implementation of a program and provide a way to invite them to become active participants.

• *Formal Presentations.* The development of slide programs or recordings can be valuable in informing members of the school community about a parent program. One advantage of this method is the use of photos or conversations of participants from previous programs to inform and "sell" potential new programs. When people recognize friends, neighbors, or other members of the community, the credibility of the parent program is enhanced considerably.

• *Gatherings.* Assemblies or formal speeches to community organizations are another way of informing the public about a specific parent program. Neighborhood or block organizations are potential audiences for spreading the word about a program and inviting individuals to participate. Making a presentation on "friendly turf" also enhances its reception as well as its desirability.

Publicizing and promoting parent programs in reading must be essential ingredients in the implementation phase of a project. It is important to tell parents and the community at large about a special program to enlist their support and involvement. Such efforts help make reading achievement a concern not only to educators, but of every citizen as well.

Chapter Three
Selected Parent Programs

Studies have made it clear that parental involvement of different kinds and degrees in a child's reading program usually results in significant gains that otherwise would not have occurred (Burgess, 1982; Hickey, 1979; Siders & Sledjeski, 1978; Vukelich 1978; Vukelich & Naeny, 1980). As a result, an increasing number of schools are taking on the function of providing practical and effective ways that parents can play a role in the instructional process of reading. The responsibility for planning and initiating this partnership most often rests with the classroom teacher or reading specialist. Both must be ready to present parents with either entire programs or separate activities that reinforce formal school instruction.

There are many project ideas that can help bring educators and parents together within the reading curriculum. This chapter describes a variety of programs that have been initiated in a number of educational settings. They are offered here in order to give the reader an overview of the wide range of actual projects that can be and have been effective. The programs are divided into three categories: Home Oriented, School Oriented, and Comprehensive programs. These classifications are not rigid, since some programs can share characteristics of more than one design. Rather, the intent is to offer a sampling of possibilities that exist for these three different approaches to parent programs.

Home Oriented Programs

Programs of this design provide home based reading activities that encourage parents and children to interact in a positive and reinforcing learning environment. Home instructional materials and projects are those which are usually separate from regular homework assignments. The information given to parents may include simple strategies and activities designed to be used away from the school and to provide everyday sharing experiences that are fun.

1. *Parent Involvement Packets.* Parents often want to help their children at home, but are not always confident of the materials and methods they should use.

This individualized program uses a special pocket portfolio sent home on a regular basis for each student in a class. Based upon a diagnosis of each pupil's reading strengths and weaknesses, a variety of activities and projects is selected for home reinforcement. Included in each packet are workbook exercises, games, puzzles, cassette tapes, and individually selected books to share. These materials may be those currently in use in other classrooms, available in a teacher center in the school, purchased from a local teacher supply store, created by groups of parents and teachers, or obtained with funds donated by the school's parent-teacher organization.

The packets can be assembled once every two weeks by teams of students. Several classroom committees can be responsible for gathering, collating, and stuffing each individual packet — a practice that can help to ensure greater participation for both parents and students. Included with each packet can be a special sheet for the recording of a teacher's comments and a place for parents' signatures. Upon completion of the activities, the packets are signed and returned for the next two week cycle.

2. *Parents As Reading Partners.* One of the most valuable activities that parents can do with their children is to read with them on a regular basis. One way that teachers can promote the reading habit at home is by initiating a Parents As Reading Partners (PARP) program. As described in an earlier chapter, PARP is a program that encourages parents and children to read together on a regular basis. The child may read to the parent, the parent to the child, or the parent may read one book while the child reads another. Families are provided with monthly calendars on which they can record the times they read together. At the end of each month, students who have read with their parents for a specified number of days are presented with special certificates, ribbons, buttons, prizes, or awards. A new calendar is sent home to each family for the following month.

As students complete their calendar for the month, a chart or other official record can be filled in. Students then have the opportunity to note their progress in the program. At the completion of the program, pupils may receive gold seals, letters of recognition from the principal, or other appropriate honors.

3. *Summer Reading Activities Notebook.* Parents and teachers are often concerned about maintaining over the summer months the development made in reading skills. At the conclusion of the school year parents will often request a number of activities, recommended books, or reading games that can be used at home. A group of teachers and parents can be assembled to put together a reading activities notebook that families can use on summer days, on a trip, on rainy days at home, or even throughout the year. These activities, assembled into a loose leaf notebook or folder, can then be distributed to students at the start of summer vacation. Items included in the notebook could be teacher-made games, lists of suggested books,

comprehension activities, vocabulary projects, photocopied skill sheets, tips and suggestions for family sharing time, recipes for learning, newspaper activities, and tips for TV viewing. Many teacher resource books contain a wealth of activities that could be considered for inclusion. In addition, a certain number of contract sheets could be placed in each notebook. After parents and children have completed a specified number of activities, these sheets can be filled in. When the records are turned in at the beginning of the next school year, students and families would be eligible for special certificates or free books to be presented by the principal or reading specialist.

4. *School and Home Activities for Reading Enrichment (*SHARE*).* This program reinforces classroom reading through parent activities that are based on stories read regularly in class. For each book that is planned to be read to the class, a special handout can be prepared which will include a variety of follow-up activities that parents and pupils can engage in at home to extend the book even further. Included on each sheet is a selection of discussion questions relating to specific characters, settings, or actions within the story that was read. The inclusion of inferential type questions will give families the opportunity to share the book or story beyond the literal level, while at the same time fostering important thinking skills.

Each handout could also contain one or two family projects related to the book. Instructions can be included for creating a mobile of the major characters, a diorama of important scenes, a poster of significant events, or a clay model of a particular object in the book. These projects, incorporating materials commonly found in the home, can be constructed by both parents and children, providing many opportunities for sharing the contents of books read in class. By consulting any good teacher aid book for suggested activities, these projects can be adapted to the dynamics of different families. A periodic "show and tell" in class may also be a possible component of this particular project.

5. *Calendar of Reading Skills.* A monthly calendar of daily reading activities can provide daily incentive for parent-child interaction. Prior to the beginning of each month, a blank calendar page is filled in with numerous activities that families can engage in together. Keeping the activities short and simple and using common household objects (magazines, paper plates, crayons), increase the likelihood of their use. Each box for the month contains an appropriate activity or project keyed to the age or ability levels of the child involved. Duplicated and distributed at the beginning of the month, each activity should be initialed by parents as it is completed. An additional feature of this project would be to schedule a series of correlated workshops that would provide parents with assistance in using the calendars and in reinforcing the basic skills. Calendars could be designed for one class, a whole grade level, a school, or several schools within a district.

6. *Parent Newsletter.* Periodic newsletters have been a common means of com-

munication between school and home for many years. Typically, newsletters offer parents a selection of learning games, reading tips and ideas, a skill sheet, or other appropriate reading suggestions. Consideration could also be given to having a group of parents write, edit and distribute newsletters for a class, school or district. Rotating the assignments among several committees can add variety to the routine and help keep a freshness in the project.

The following are possibilities for inclusion in various issues:

- Informal reading sources (cereal boxes, TV schedule).
- A question and answer section for specific parent concerns.
- A recipe corner ("Following Directions").
- Suggestions for specific children's magazines.
- Inclusion of children's work (poems, stories, drawings).
- The value of reading with one's child regularly.
- Suggested children's books.
- A letter from the principal or reading specialist.
- Places to go, things to do in and around the local community.
- A listing of upcoming stories in the basal text.
- The value of talking with one's child; positive communication.
- Happenings at the local library.
- Upcoming educational programs on TV.
- A featured children's author or illustrator.
- A simple reading game or two.
- Special reading selections or books for parents.
- Guest columnists (librarian, mayor, superintendent).
- Suggestions for how to read aloud to one's child.

7. *Other Possibilities.* On a less ambitious scale are these suggestions for helping parents to create purposeful language experiences for their children as well as to encourage their reading. For example, in the "Tote-a-Book" program children take home a self-selected book on their independent reading level, and with their parents complete special report forms (Washington Elementary School, Tipton, Indiana). A traveling neighborhood storyteller can bring language enrichment during playtime or other relaxed times. Neighborhood field trips to printers or newspapers can emphasize the importance of language in our world. Taped stories circulated among parents provide reinforcement of silent reading skills and also have the value of being a different way to read. In a Book-of-the-Month Club, families recommend favorite books for a monthly list of titles distributed to all. Though not as comprehensive as the other home programs, these projects can be important adjuncts to reading instruction as well as provide a low key beginning for parental involvement.

School Oriented Programs

The programs described in this section emphasize onsite services provided by the school to meet the needs of parents. These school based activities are learning opportunities designed to increase the parents' effectiveness in influencing their child's reading development. Projects may also focus on offerings at a central facility apart from the school such as the YMCA or church.

1. *After School Workshops.* Many schools have found that one of the best ways to provide parents with information that they can use to work with their children is by scheduling a series of workshops. These sessions, set up either in the evening or on the weekend, can offer parents the opportunity to view and create a wide variety of learning activities and games for their youngsters. The "make-and-take" approach has many advantages, not the least of which is that it provides parents with first hand experiences in developing learning projects specifically geared for the ability and interests of their children. Additionally, when the entire family has an opportunity to participate together, the concept of reading as a family activity can be cultivated. Another advantage is that workshops involve parents and educators together in an informal atmosphere, helping to establish good rapport between home and school.

2. *Family Reading Center.* Offering parents specific materials correlated to the school's reading program can be a valuable means of engaging parents in the reading development of their children. Schools often have a selection of duplicate materials or extra supplies than can be sent home on a regular basis. Extra skill sheets, reading games or puzzles, publisher's samples, or other reading aids can be located and arranged in a classroom or the school's central office. Cataloged and matched to the skills taught in the basal text, these materials can be made available to families as part of the total reading program. Families should be invited to check out these items so that they may be used at home. Beside putting to good use all possible reading materials in the school, this type of project provides parents with a selection of reading materials that they might not otherwise have at home.

3. *Open House.* Providing parents with informal as well as formal opportunities to interact with school personnel can have many important advantages for the overall reading program. Arrangements can be made whereby parents are invited to the school in the morning to observe the reading program in action. A simple checklist given to visitors can tell them of the instructional objectives taught as well as the activities normally scheduled. Parents should be invited to more than one classroom and not necessarily only those of their children. After the visit, they may join the principal or reading specialist for a brown bag lunch or an informal coffee hour in order to discuss various aspects of the reading program. An open luncheon for parents could also be scheduled on a weekly basis, providing a time when their questions or concerns about the reading program can be addressed.

An additional feature of this program would be to provide each parent with a book, reading game or take home activity to share with their children. A follow-up letter of thanks would also be appropriate.

4. *Reading Advisory Council.* Inviting parents to participate in the design and implementation of the reading program can have many positive benefits, especially in generating their support and enthusiasm for what happens in the classroom. A reading council composed of equal numbers of parents and educators can be established within an individual school or across an entire district. The responsibility of the council would be to develop strategies to improve the overall design of the reading program as well as to keep the community informed about continuing or special reading activities. The use of ongoing needs assessment strategies would provide the council with valuable information upon which to base their recommendations and decisions. Another advantage of this type of council is that it offers a direct link to parents in the community concerning various facets of the reading program, particularly if parents from different grade levels and socioeconomic groups are enlisted. Ensuring a diversity of voices will also increase the chances for the council's recommendations to be heard and acted upon.

5. *Reading Conference for Parents.* Based upon a needs assessment, it may be discovered that there are many areas of reading for which parents need additional information. A committee of parents and teachers can be organized specifically to develop a school or district-wide reading conference for parents. Arrangements could be made to set aside one school day during the year when families can come to a central location to attend a series of workshops, discussion sessions, or presentations on various reading topics. Speakers or presenters could include local or outside classroom teachers, reading specialists, college teachers, publishers' representatives, librarians, or other reading related people. If the conference is aimed at the entire family, it may also offer a variety of activities for children (babysitting service, game making, educational films, library time).

6. *Parent Reading Course.* As part of the school district's adult education, a special course for parents could be designed and developed. Offered by some of the teachers in the district, this course could focus on how parents can work with their children at home, describe family activities that reinforce reading instruction, provide family book lists for different grade levels, or present an overview of the district's reading curriculum. Including a variety of activities, demonstrations, discussions, and guest speakers will be the keys to success of any course. Needs assessment would indicate the appropriate length of the course, its content, and times for meeting. A number of child related individuals (nurses, pediatricians, psychologists, guidance counselors) could be asked to present and respond to parental concerns.

7. *Other Possibilities.* Less intricate activities include a Pot Luck Dinner for families invited to school for a covered dish dinner. An after dinner program might feature a speaker, miniworkshop, slide-tape presentation or other activities that focus on enriching the parents' skills. In a "Parent Outreach Program," a special group prepares packets of activities, games, and worksheets for parents who are unable to come to school. Its organization can be like that of the "Meals on Wheels" program. Some schools might consider providing recorded messages on the school's answering system or other simple devices to stimulate parental involvement in their child's learning.

Comprehensive Programs

These projects are designed to engage the family in a multifaceted program of home and school interaction. Typically, a combination of home based and school based components are used in order to provide a selection of services for parents. These projects may include training workshops, informational materials, home visits, home use materials, community outreach services, and parent support groups.

1. *Volunteer Programs.* A widely used method for helping parents become involved in the classroom activities of the reading program is by enlisting their aid as classroom volunteers. Besides providing teachers with assistance, volunteers view firsthand the workings of the school's reading program. By doing so they gain a better appreciation of how it affects their children and, just as importantly, how they can participate in that process. Their assistance can be helpful in many different areas of the reading program; however, their value will be ultimately determined by how well they are trained prior to placement in the classroom. It is essential that a comprehensive inservice training program provide volunteers with the skills and attitudes necessary to assist youngsters in the best way possible.

Some of the activities that volunteers can perform in the classroom may include listening regularly to youngsters read selected stories from the basal or their library books. Checklists of potential errors may also be appropriate for this activity. Volunteers could offer individualized instruction to small groups of students who may be experiencing some difficulty with a certain reading skill. Also, volunteers can provide home services to those families who find it difficult to come to school. By matching the skills taught in the classroom to materials sent out with these volunteers, the reading program could become a powerful home/school venture.

2. *Books Are for Sharing.* Parents often ask about the kinds of books that may be appropriate for their children. A "Books Are for Sharing" program can provide parents with a selection of children's books geared to the interests and abilities of their youngsters. The program would also provide parents and children different

ways to share and talk about books, including reading books together, listening to tape recordings of books, and silent reading sessions. The books should be selected and cataloged according to interest inventories completed by each child at the beginning of the school year. A specially designed series of questions for families to share could accompany each book. In addition, special project cards can be provided for each book to allow parents and children the opportunity to create posters, dioramas, murals, and mobiles of the characters and scenes in a book. These activities would allow families to extend the reading experience beyond the printed page. "Books Are for Sharing" can evolve into an extension of the basal reading program in addition to providing children and parents with an enjoyable way to share good literature.

3. *Parents As Partners in Reading* (PAPIR). Many parents are responsive to programs that provide them with reading information when their children enter school for the first time. A special project can be developed to offer parents of kindergarten students information on the activities and guidelines that contribute to the positive reading development of young children. The project may consist of several interrelated components: 1) a series of workshop sessions scheduled throughout the year which focus on a basic understanding of how children learn to read, several hands-on activities that parents can use at home, a variety of games to reinforce prereading skills, and a brainstorming session to air common concerns and questions; 2) a handbook of practical suggestions and ideas about reading to children, providing worthwhile experiences, motivating them to read, and other helpful hints; 3) a monthly newsletter containing tips on specific reading activities parents and children can share at home; 4) learning packets containing parent-made games and activities; and 5) a small, free library of selected children's books appropriate for storytelling and sharing. This project can provide parents with the concepts and methods they may need to promote the initial reading development of their children.

4. *Community News Service.* Many community newspapers must look for news items to fill their pages. A group of educators and parents can be organized to develop and submit a regular column to the local paper. This column could contain hints and tips on how parents can take an active role in their children's reading development, information on reading programs or events scheduled for the community, or a question and answer section which would solicit and respond to questions of parents.

If a specific community does not have its own newspaper or if the city paper is unresponsive to a group's requests, it may be possible to develop an insert which could be distributed with the regular paper. In any event, contacts in the local media can have many benefits, including helping public relations for subsequent parent programs in reading.

5. *Reading Awareness Week.* To bring the community and school closer, a special week can be designated, perhaps through a proclamation from the mayor, as "Reading Awareness Week." Activities during that time could include a parade of storybook characters around town, providing doctors' offices with selections of books and tips for parents, storytelling sessions scheduled at a local shopping center, visiting children's authors and other outside speakers, promotion of the local library, and other activities designed to demonstrate the community's support of parental involvement in reading.

6. *Family Reading Fair.* Usually scheduled for a weekend at a local shopping mall, these events have sprung up in locations coast to coast from Newport News, Virginia, to San Mateo County, California. They provide the opportunity for educators and community members to come together and promote a common goal.

The Fair, designed to involve parents and children in fun-filled and hands-on reading experiences, can present a variety of activities and displays. Included could be reading games, story times, computer learning projects, roving storybook characters, puppet shows, information booths, school displays, community outreach groups, professional consultations, prizes, awards and book giveaways.

Although an event of this nature requires a great deal of coordinated effort, it does stimulate a greater awareness of parental influence on children's reading growth. Further, it has the potential to establish lines of communication between educational and community groups.

7. *Other Possibilities.* Projects which do not require as much time or money include "Dial-A-Teacher"—a hotline that provides parents with assistance on their children's homework assignments (United Federation of Teachers, New York). Taped programs that offer reading tips for parents could be distributed to local libraries, school systems, reading councils, and community organizations (North Jersey Council of IRA). Departments of Education at local colleges and university are often delighted when their majors can present workshops, miniconferences, or make visits. A van, converted into a bookmobile, could make periodic visits to neighborhoods to provide books, pamphlets, or miniworkshops.

Summary

In addition to the programs described, the most effective ones are probably those that have not yet been thought of. The best ideas will be those that are born of the needs of a specific group and tailored to the resources and talents available. An important part of making any parent program work is the creative vision and drive that surround all of its parts. That energy comes most easily and naturally when the concept is a personal one. Readers are encouraged to consider the programs as models and as proof that important, valuable work with parents is possible if you are willing to plan, work, and to dream.

Appendix Guide

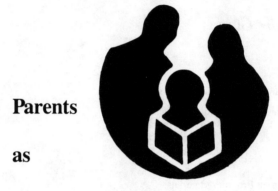

Parents

as

Reading Partners

SHECKLER ELEMENTARY SCHOOL

Dear Parents:

I invite you to join our new "Parents as Reading Partners" program. It's a great way to help your child learn good reading habits. And it's so easy to participate—there's no money to spend and there are no trips to take. All you have to do is spend 15 minutes each day reading with your child.

And as you read with your child, keep a record on the *Parents as Reading Partners Contract* sent home with your child each month. This record will help your child earn special awards as well as a final "Program Certificate" at the end of the year (suitable for framing). More details about our recognition program are on the back of this folder.

Remember, you are your child's best teacher. Reading with him or her each day can mean a great deal in forming lifelong reading habits.

Thank you for your help.

Sincerely,

Reading Specialist

TIPS FOR PARENTS

Here's how you can help your child:

Turn off the TV set. Its noise can be distracting.

With younger children, look at picture books and tell stories.

As your child begins to read, help him or her pick books of interest.

After reading a book, talk about it together.

Visit the library with your child often.

Let your child see you enjoying a book, magazine, or newspaper.

Spend at least 15 minutes a day reading with your child. EVERY DAY.

Parents
as
Reading Partners

PARENTS AS READING PARTNERS
Student Recognition Program

Monthly Awards

Each month of the *Parents as Reading Partners* Program, special awards will be given to children who read with a parent for *15 minutes* on *at least 20 days* during that month.

For your child to receive the award, please complete that month's *Parents as Reading Partners Contract/Calendar* and have the student take it to his or her teacher at the end of the month. Your child will then receive a new contract/calendar for the next month.

Program Achievement Certificate

At the end of the year, children who have read with a parent for *15 minutes* on at least *20 different days each month* for *8 months* will receive a distinctive achievement certificate (suitable for framing).

Special Features

During the year there will be special awards and recognition for students and parents in the *Parents as Reading Partners* Program. Reading Family of the Month, special newsletters, newspaper reports, free books and bookmarkers, a book exchange, an awards assembly, and classroom sharing time will be some of the special features of the program for your child. Please help to share this valuable experience with your children.

PARENTS AS READING PARTNERS CONTRACT
Read 15 minutes every day

SUN	MON	TUES	WEDS	THURS	FRI	SAT

OUR CONTRACT

I hereby promise to listen (or read) to my child (children) at home every day for 15 minutes during the month of _____ .

_____
Parent's Name (Please Print)

My child's name is _____

Parents: 1) Put a ✓ mark in a box for each day you and your child read together for at least 15 minutes.

2) You may wish to write in the dates for this month.

3) Have your child return the completed calendar to his/her teacher at the end of the month.

4) If you and your child read together for a minimum of 20 days this month, your child will receive a special certificate

Fredericks and Taylor

Certificate of Merit

SHECKLER ELEMENTARY SCHOOL

PARENTS AS READING PARTNERS

This certifies that _____ and family have read together on a regular basis during the months indicated and are hereby awarded this certificate of merit.

Presented this _____ *day of* _____ , 19 _____

_____
Teacher

_____
Principal

OCT.

NOV.

DEC.

JAN.

FEB.

MAR.

APR.

MAY

trashable — an item that is usually thrown away; JUNK.

Did you Know that you can make learning games from inexpensive or throw away items? Attend the parent child workshop and find out how!

Place _____

Time _____

Date _____

Start collecting these materials and bring them with you to the workshop: egg cartons, pretzel or chip cans, L'eggs eggs, styrofoam and/or paper plates, clean bleach bottles, cottage cheese and yogurt containers, large paper bags, ziploc bags (small), scissors, one fine point permanent magic marker.

Yes, we are interested in attending the "make and take" workshop.

Parents name _____
Child's name _____
Total number of persons attending _____

P.A.P.I.R.

PARENTS AS PARTNERS IN READING
SHECKLER ELEMENTARY SCHOOL

Dear Parents:

I would like to take this oportunity to welcome you to Sheckler Elementary School and specifically to the kindergarten program your child will attend next fall. We sincerely hope that your child's first contact with formal education will be a rich and rewarding experience and one that will start him/her on the road to academic success.

In order to help give your child the experiences that lead to *reading* success we would like to tell you about a new program — the P.A.P.I.R. project. The goal of this project will be to help you become aware of, and provide you with, activities and suggestions that contribute to the reading development of your child. It is important that you as a parent understand the role you play in your child's educational development, as well as the activities you can use to promote that development.

The P.A.P.I.R. project will be conducted during the entire school year, beginning in the fall, and will consist of workshop sessions, handbooks, newsletters, guest speakers, free books, and other activities designed to help you help your child to learn to read. Due to space and material limitations only 45 parents will be able to participate in the program (23 from a.m. kindergarten; 22 from p.m.). There will be no costs involved; however, we would require participants to come into school (either in the morning or afternoon) for six workshop sessions during the year.

The following pages will give you additional information on the P.A.P.I.R. project. If you are interested in participating in the project in the fall or would just like to get more information, please fill in the form in the back of this booklet and return it to me at Sheckler. If you have any questions concerning the project, please feel free to call me at school (264-5601).

Again, welcome to an exciting new beginning for your child.

Sincerely,

Reading Specialist

The following P.A.P.I.R. project activities, scheduled throughout the year, are designed to involve parents in the reading development of their children.

1. Parents in the project will participate in six workshop sessions of 2½ hours each (see following page). There will be one session in September, three in October, one in January, and one in May. Parents whose children attend a.m. kindergarten classes will participate in morning sessions; parents whose children attend p.m. classes will participate in afternoon sessions of the program.

2. A handbook of practical suggestions will be given to each parent in the program. It will contain ideas on reading to children and provide worthwhile experiences, motivation techniques, effects of TV, and other helpful information.

3. A monthly newsletter will be distributed to all participants. These newsletters will contain timely tips and suggestions on specific reading activities that parents and children can share at home.

4. Parents will be given "Learning Packages" which will consist of a tote bag filled with reading games and activities geared to the ability and interests of each child. Parents and children will be able to work on these activities at home.

5. Each parent will be given a free "Library" of children's books (approximately 25) selected by the reading specialist as appropriate for kindergarten children. These books will include children's "classics" appropriate for storytelling and sharing.

Each of the six workshop sessions (2½ hours each) will be composed of the following parts:

A. *Discussion.* This will consist of an informal presentation by the reading specialist on two informational topics for parents. Each discussion will be designed to provide background information necessary to an understanding of the child's role in the reading process (time-30 minutes).

    Examples: 1) How children learn to read
                 2) Kindergarten children and reading readiness

B. *Activities.* This segment will consist of "hands-on" experiences and special materials that parents can use in their daily contracts with their children (time-30 minutes).

    Examples: 1) How to read to your child
                 2) Sharing of recommended book lists

C. *Games.* Parents will be given the opportunity to construct games that reinforce prereading skills. Using common household objects (egg cartons, cans, buttons, etc.), parents will be able to make learning games in line with their children's individual needs (time-1 hour).

    Examples: 1) "Letter Lotto"
                 2) "Word Bingo"

D. *Brainstorming.* As a follow up to each session, parents will have a chance to share common concerns, needs, and problems with the reading specialist. Participants will be able to arrive at mutually satisfying solutions and directions (time-30 minutes).

    Examples: 1) "What if my child isn't interested in learning to read?"
                 2) "How do I help my child if I work all day?"

BENEFITS FOR YOUR CHILD

Your child will benefit from your participation in the P.A.P.I.R. project in the following ways:

1) Your child will receive, free of charge, a collection of paperback books suitable for primary level students. These books will help him/her start a "first library"—something which can be treasured for years to come.

2) Your child will be able to experience a number of prereading games that you have made specifically for him/her. Your child will find these games to be both entertaining and educational.

3) Your child will be able to experience a wide variety of words through a number of learning activities designed to help children acquire rich vocabularies.

4) Students and parents participating in the P.A.P.I.R. project will be allowed to use the Sheckler School Library. Each student will be given a specially designed library card which may be used to check out books from the library. A special section of the library will be designated for prereading books. The librarian, the reading specialist, and parents will assist children in obtaining books.

5) Students will be active participants in the program by keeping track of the number of books they and their parents share during the year. Students become eligible for special awards as they progress through the program.

6) At the conclusion of the program children will be invited to participate in a "reading party." Pupils will be able to share their experiences with books, receive participant certificates, obtain additional books, and share in a variety of reading games.

7) Above all, children will be offered experiences that will help them grow and develop into competent readers. Parents, teachers, and children working together will help to insure reading success for all participating students.

The home environment is an important factor in helping children learn to read. A child's ability to learn positive reading habits is affected to some degree by his/her experiences at home. As a result, parents can help provide an atmosphere that will encourage reading growth in their children.

The following suggestions will help you in helping your child prepare for reading success:

1) Talk to your child. This is important since the more words he/she hears, then the more words he/she will be able to use in ordinary conversation. As a result, words will have more meaning for him/her when seen on the printed page.

2) Listen to your child. It is important for children to have opportunities to express themselves. The more a child talks, and the more it is appreciated, then the better he/she will be able to develop adequate language patterns.

3) Read to your child. Every time you read to your child you are developing an appreciation of books as well as of reading. You are also reinforcing an understanding of the relationship between spoken and written language. The child who has been read to will undoubtedly be anxious to read for himself/herself.

4) Help develop your child's growth in vocabulary. Vocabulary growth can be helped by an exploration of your child's environment. Have him/her ask questions about the surroundings and then answer them. Supply labels and descriptions to various parts of his/her world. Make sure these new words have meaning by using them in a contextual arrangement—that is, by talking *with* your child (not to him/her) about them.

5) Have him/her become aware of sounds: Their differences and similarities. You may wish to start off by tapping with a spoon glasses filled to different levels with water. Say three words all with the same initial sound; add a fourth with a completely different sound. Develop games utilizing animal sounds, house sounds, people sounds, etc. These will help your child to discriminate between sounds and perhaps encourage him/her to make some too.

6) Help your child develop visual skills. Point out differences in color, size, shape, form, and position of things around the house and in the neighborhood. A variety of games can be developed in order to help your child develop good visual skills.

Fredericks and Taylor

7) Provide your child with activities for doing things and going places. The development of a wide range of experiences will help your child attain good comprehension of written material later in his or her academic career. Point out interesting things around you and give your child new words and meanings for words.

8) Build up a reading atmosphere at home. Have books, magazines, newspapers, etc. around the house. The position of reading material and reading at home is important to your child's appreciation of reading. Parents should be readers themselves, and if they enjoy reading, it is likely that children will enjoy reading as well.

9) Buy games and puzzles for your child. These can help your child learn shapes and forms, to help him/her relate words to things. Anagrams, jigsaw puzzles, letter games, Scrabble and Lotto all contribute to the development of spelling and reading skills.

10) Buy books for your child. For birthdays, holidays, or for any occasion, buy books when you can afford them. Interest in reading can be stimulated by ownership of a few good books.

Parents should remember that there is no magic formula for preparing a child for reading. The emphasis should be on the creation of a relaxed atmosphere in order to give your child the time necessary to absorb and understand the activities used. Each child will, of course, learn at his/her own rate. Parents, then, should be ready to guide their children toward reading development and success, and help them see all the joy and wonderment associated with learning to read.

☐ Yes, I am interested in the P.A.P.I.R project. Send me more
  information in the fall.

Child's name _____

Parent'(s) name _____

Address _____

_____

Phone _____

Best time to call _____

Father's occupation   Mother's occupation

_____   _____

Working hours   Working hours

_____   _____

Comments:

Fredericks and Taylor

"READING IS A FAMILY AFFAIR"

Sheckler Elementary School

Dear Parents:

Welcome to a new year of learning at Sheckler. We are looking forward to a rich variety of successful educational experiences for all our students. In order that we may help your child(ren) grow and learn in reading we would like to invite you to participate in some exciting programs designed especially for you.

We sincerely believe that parents can play a most important role in their children's academic development. For this reason we have developed a variety of parent participation programs in reading designed to help your child succeed. These programs are designed for every parent and every family. It's very easy to particiapte — there's no cost involved, only a little bit of your time.

On the following pages of this booklet you will discover a selection of parent progams and projects in reading developed with you and your child(ren) in mind. We sincerely hope that you and your family will take advantage of these offerings and help us promote reading success for all students at Sheckler.

If you have any questions or concerns about any of these programs please feel free to contact me at any time. If we can provide you with any special services or help you in any way to help your child grow in reading, we are always ready to assist you.

Sincerely,

Reading Specialist

SHECKLER
HOME HELP
PROGRAM

The Home Help Program is designed to provide you with specific reading materials, techniques, and instructions to help you help your child(ren) develop reading competence. It was initiated on the premise that parents can and should be active partners in the learning process of their children.

The Home Help Program will reinforce regular classroom reading instruction by providing you with reading materials and games, advice on their use, and the opportunity to check them out and use them with your child at home. The program is developed around 27 specific skill areas in reading. These skills are grouped in the following areas: phonic analysis, structural analysis, vocabulary, and comprehension. The materials available in the Home Help Program are keyed to these skill areas as well as coded to specific grade levels and correlated with our basal reading program.

A Diagnostic Analysis Card is kept on file for each child in the school. This will assure you that the materials selected will be those your child needs for reading competence. Both your child's teacher and the reading specialist will continuously update these cards to insure a cooperative effort in maximizing reading growth. You can be assured that your child's progress will be accurately monitored and that individual materials will be available for every reading skill your child encounters in the classroom.

We invite you to come into the Family Reading Center located on the first floor of Sheckler near the first grade classrooms and obtain materials specifically designed for your child. The Center will be open during the following times: Tuesdays, 8:30-12:30; Wednesdays, 11:30-3:30; Thursdays, 8:30-12:30.

FAMILY READING FAIR

In order to provide parents and families with valuable information on their children, reading specialists from the Catasauqua and East Penn School Districts in cooperation with educators from almost every school in the Lehigh Valley have organized and planned the *Family Reading Fair* to be held on

---

Saturday, Nov. 7 – 10:00 A.M. - 6:00 P.M. – Lehigh Valley Mall

---

The *Family Reading Fair* is specifically designed to
A. Help parents and community members:
  • Become more aware of their role in promoting positive reading attitudes.
  • Better understand the reading process and how they may help their children.
  • Better understand their role in supporting reading as a lifetime habit.
B. Provide children with:
  • The opportunity to participate in a wide range of creative reading activities.
  • Activities to help promote reading as a worthwhile and interesting habit.
Some of the events planned for the fair include:
  1. Parent information booths – take home pamphlets, brochures
  2. Strolling storybook characters
  3. Professionals from a variety of educational fields
  4. Displays of educational games
  5. Popular children's authors
  6. Preschool activities booths
  7. Storybook room
  8. Bookmaking activities
  9. Slide/tape shows of parent-child reading experiences
  10. Puppet shows, guest stars, prizes, awards, books, and lots more

BOOKS
ARE
FOR
SHARING

The "Books Are for Sharing" program was established to provide you with a wide variety of suitable children's books geared to the interests and ability of your child(ren). Individual Interest Inventories are given to each child in the school to determine the specific reading interests of each individual. Your child can select interests from adventure to sports and from animal stories to science fiction. These inventories are then kept in the *Family Reading Center* and are filed by grade level and classroom teacher.

Over 1500 paperback books are catalogued in the Family Reading Center according to the following criteria:

1. Specific interests of students in grades 1-4
2. Specific reading levels of individual students

You and your child will have the opportunity to check out these books and a) read them together, b) listen to a recording of each book, c) read the book to your child, d) have your child read the book to you, or e) have your child read the book silently on his or her own.

In addition you and your child will be provided with a series of discussion questions specifically designed for each book. These questions will permit you and your child to share ideas and work on the comprehension and understanding of stories. Additionally, you will also be given a list of activities for each book that you and your child can share together. Projects such as creating a mobile of the main characters, making a poster of the book's setting, working on a diorama of certain events, or creating a puppet of the hero or heroine will be outlined. These activities will provide your youngster with interesting "hands on" experiences with children's literature. Plan to stop by the Family Reading Center and check us out.

COFFEE 'N READING

Coffee 'N Reading is a program designed to provide parents with the activities, games, and suggestions that will contribute to their children's positive experiences with reading. Organized in cooperation with the Sheckler Home & School Association and the Parent Advisory Council of the district's Title I Reading Program, *Coffee 'N Reading* consists of a series of monthly workshops scheduled throughout the school year.

> November 19
> December 15
> January 20
> February 11
> March 19
> April 20
> May 14

These workshops will be held in room 205 from 9:00-12:00 on the dates indicated. As a parent you will have an opportunity to:

1) discuss your child's reading program with the reading specialist;
2) make and prepare specific projects that you and your child can share at home;
3) receive valuable tips and suggestions on motivating your child to read; and
4) discuss problems, concerns, or questions and obtain information specifically for your child.

Fredericks and Taylor

Selected Parent Activities

Note: This list is not meant to be a complete catalog of specific activities. Its purpose is to suggest ways of finding activities and of generating parents' involvement in their child's reading development.

1. Adapt for parent use some of the activities found in teacher aid books. Many of the games, puzzles, and projects can be modified for home use with common household objects.

2. Send home lists of recommended children's books. Lists provided by the ALA or Children's Book Council offer parents a selection of books available at both the local library and area bookstores. Parents need to feel confident that they are choosing good books for their children, and such a list can act as a catalyst for a trip to the library.

3. Provide parents with weekly or biweekly notes on upcoming stories in the basal text. Offer a selection of questions or discussion points that parents can share with their children.

4. Help students to write an occasional letter to parents outlining an activity or two that can be shared at home. Photocopy those letters and distribute them to all families. Make sure that all pupils have an opportunity to create two or three letters during the year.

5. Send parents a calendar of reading activities for family use. Using a blank calendar page, write in several games or projects that children and parents can share at home. Solicit ideas from all the students.

6. Obtain complimentary samples of children's books from publishers or book distributors. Send these home with children on a regular basis with a short note to parents including several sharing activities.

7. Devote an entire day to a "Celebration of Reading." Invite parents to join with students in sharing a variety of activities and projects centered around reading. There could be a make-and-take workshop, a silent reading time, group reading games, book sharing projects, or classroom discussions based on popular quiz

shows. This classroom based project also could emphasize the variety of activities that parents and children do at home.

8. Schedule a day or a week when the only reading material parents and students are "allowed" to read is the daily newspaper. Write up a series of daily activities in which families can participate together and reinforce them with special activities in the classroom. Plan all the subject area lessons around the newspaper, too (pupils may find it enjoyable to use just the newspaper as their "textbooks" for an entire week).

9. Ask families to create special reading projects based on popular book characters or themes. Posters, dioramas, and shadow boxes are projects that parents and kids can do at home. Schedule a day when families can come to school to share their various creations. You may want to enliven the proceedings by requiring everyone to come dressed as their favorite storybook character.

10. If possible, you may wish to travel to parents' homes at least once during the year to offer them a selection of popular books, handouts, or other activities in which families can participate together. This kind of face-to-face contact offers many advantages in establishing a positive home/school relationship.

11. Keep track of upcoming TV or programs or movies. Provide parents with lists of books or other reading selections that tie in with these shows. Many popular children's books have been developed into television programs, particularly those shown as after school specials. Help parents use TV as a medium to promote reading skills.

12. Provide parents and children with specific directions for creating their own books. There are several children's books which describe the methods and materials appropriate for self-made books. Offer parents some instructions on developing appropriate language experience stories about going to the zoo, making popcorn balls, or other common experiences, and how they can be turned into actual books. Schedule a "show and tell" day for all the books to be displayed.

13. Solicit ideas from parents on some of the reading activities and projects they have used at home and have found to be fun and motivating. Collect these ideas into a booklet for distribution to all parents in the class or the school. If enough ideas are collected, they can be used in several newsletters as well.

14. Work with students in creating a variety of games and projects that can be used over the summer months. Collect these into several folders and distribute to all families just prior to summer vacation.

15. Work with the local library to develop a series of workshops or special parent meetings that offer ideas and strategies to families on reading development. A cooperative effort could include distribution of a list of newly released books, special children's films keyed to popular books, or special visits by the bookmobile to local neighborhoods with teachers, librarians, and students distributing the books.

Fredericks and Taylor

16. Families may want to assemble a "Family Reading Scrapbook" including photos of family members reading silently, lists of popular books, activities, and games that have been played at home, or other special occurrences. The emphasis would be on developing a variety of reading activities and helping families understand the many projects that can contribute to good reading development. These scrapbooks may be brought into school to be shared and discussed by the students.

17. Call parents frequently to offer them ideas and activities that promote home reading. Often the telephone is used to relay bad news; however, it also can be a way to share supportive activities and projects that extend classroom reading instruction.

18. Regularly offer parents a selection of specific reading activities that they can do at home with their children. The following list presents only a very brief selection of endless possibilities that can be offered.

- Read to your child. Expose him or her to the variety of literature in books, stories, and poetry. (Parents may appreciate a list of do's and don'ts for reading with their children.)
- Look through books or the newspaper to locate items that have similar qualities and those that are different.
- Pick up some jigsaw puzzles from the toy store and help your child assemble them.
- Read a story to your child but leave out an occasional word. Ask your child to supply a word that makes sense.
- Make up some word or picture cards and play a game of "Concentration" with your child.
- Write several letters on index cards and ask your child to assemble them into words.
- Put your child in charge of a family calendar, recording and keeping track of family events.
- If there is a typewriter at home, provide your child with opportunities to use it, perhaps to copy sentences from a favorite story.
- Have your child locate favorite pictures in old magazines. Ask him or her to cut them out and provide captions for each one.
- Take some time to sing songs or nursery rhymes with your child. Ask your child to repeat favorite children's songs to you.
- Cut out comic strips from the newspaper and ask your child to place the "boxes" in the correct order.
- Work with your child in creating a picture dictionary using pictures from old magazines or newspapers.
- As you are driving with your child, point out things along the road and ask your child to identify the first or last letter of each item.

• Ask your child for words that he or she would like to learn. Write these on index cards and have your child place them alphabetically in a special box.

• Have your child collect special words in a folder. Ask him or her to use one of these new words each day in a sentence.

• As you read a story to your child, record it on cassette tape. Your child may want to listen to the story again at a later date.

• As you are preparing a meal, ask your child to help by reading portions of the recipes or creating a special menu.

• Before the family takes a trip, involve your child in helping with preparations — a list of items to take, specific directions on a map, or writing for travel brochures.

• Read a story to your child and ask him/her to make up a new title.

• Read part of a story to your child but omit the ending. Ask your child to develop a new ending.

• Ask your child lots of "Why?" questions, not only about the stories he/she reads but also about everyday occurrences in the home or neighborhood.

• Provide your child with a subscription to a children's magazine or to a children's book club.

• As you are watching TV with your child, ask him/her to predict the ending to a particular program.

• Ask your child about his/her favorite part of a book or story he/she has just read.

• Use the newspaper as a reading textbook. Ask your child to locate specific articles in various sections of the paper.

• Help your child start some sort of collection that can provide an opportunity for categorizing, labeling, and perhaps some informal research.

References

AULT, LYNDA. *Promising Practices: Elementary Reading Criteria for Excellence.* Juneau: Alaska State Department of Education, 1976.

BURGESS, JOANNE. "The Effects of a Training Program for Parents of Preschoolers on the Children's School Readiness," *Reading Improvement* (1982), *19*, 313-318.

CONNECTICUT STATE DEPARTMENT OF EDUCATION. *Connecticut Right to Read Program Planning Model.* Hartford: State Department of Education, 1976.

CRUZ, NORBERTO, NANCY HOLLAND, & MONICA GARLINGTON. *A Catalog of Parent Involvement Projects: A Collection of Quality Parent Projects for Assisting Children in the Achievement of Basic Skills.* Rollyn, Virginia: InterAmerica Research Associates, 1981.

DELLA-DORA, DELMO. "Parents and Other Citizens in Curriculum Development," in Ronald S. Brandt (Ed.), *Partners: Parents and Schools.* Alexandria, Virginia: Association for Supervision and Curriculum Development, 1979.

DUNCAN, PATRICIA. "Ethnography as a Methodology in the Study of the Parent Role in Reading," paper presented at the annual meeting of the College Reading Association, Boston, November 1977.

ERVIN, JANE. *How to Have a Successful Parents and Reading Program: A Practical Guide.* Boston: Allyn and Bacon, 1982.

FARLOW, HELEN. *Publicizing and Promoting Programs.* New York: McGraw-Hill, 1979.

GARDNER, ELAINE, & CATHY O'LOUGHLIN-SNYDER. "Parent Participation: The Foundation of a Successful Reading Program," paper presented at the annual convention of the International Reading Association, New Orleans, April 1981.

GRANOWSKY, ALVIN, FRANCIS R. MIDDLETON, & JANICE H. MUMFORD. "Parents as Partners in Education," *Reading Teacher,* 1979, *32,* 826-830.

HEATHINGTON, BETTY. "The Development of Scales to Measure Attitudes toward Reading," unpublished doctoral dissertation, University of Tennessee, Knoxville, 1975.

HENDERSON, ANNE. *Parent Participation — Student Achievement: The Evidence Grows.* Columbia, Maryland: National Committee for Citizens in Education, 1981.

HICKEY, KATHERINE, STEVE IMBER, & ELIZABETH RUGGIERO. "Modifying Reading Behavior of Elementary Special Needs Children: A Cooperative Resource-Parent Program," *Journal of Learning Disabilities,* 1979, *12,* 444-449.

HOME AND SCHOOL INSTITUTE. "The Families Learning Together Study," unpublished paper, Washington, D.C., 1979.

LYONS, PEGGY, DIANA DINGLER, SUSAN NERENBERG, OLGA SANDERS, & MAXINE SPARKS. *Involving Parents: A Handbook for Participation in Schools.* Santa Monica, California: System Development Corporation, 1981.

NORTH JERSEY COUNCIL OF THE INTERNATIONAL READING ASSOCIATION. Unpublished document, River Edge, New Jersey, 1982.

RICH, DOROTHY, JAMES VAN DIEN, & BEVERLY MATTOX. "Families as Educators of Their Own Children," in Ronald S. Brandt (Ed.), *Partners: Parents and Schools.* Alexandria, Virginia: Association for Supervision and Curriculum Development, 1979.

SIDERS, MARY, & STEPHEN SLEDJESKI. *How to Grow a Happy Reader: Report on a Study of Parental Involvement as it Relates to a Child's Reading Skills.* Research Monograph No. 27. Gainesville, Florida: Florida State University, 1978.

TEXAS EDUCATION AGENCY. *Criteria for Excellence for School Reading Programs.* Austin, Texas: Division of Curriculum Development, 1979.

UNITED FEDERATION OF TEACHERS. Unpublished document, New York, 1982.

VUKELICH, CAROL. "Parents Are Teachers: A Beginning Reading Program," *Reading Teacher,* 1978, *31,* 524-527.

VUKELICH, CAROL, & JOAN DYSON NAENY. "Parents as Partners in Teaching Beginning Reading: A Learning Knapsack Program," in James W. Foley (Ed.), *Parents and Reading.* New Haven, Connecticut: Connecticut Association for Reading Research, 1980.

WASHINGTON ELEMENTARY SCHOOL. Unpublished document, Tipton, Indiana, 1982.

WILLIAMS, RENEE, LYNNE KAHN, & DIANA COYLE. *Program Improvement Evaluation.* Durham, North Carolina: NTS Research Corporation, 1981.